616.83
MOE   Moe, Barbara

        Coping with Tourette
    syndrome and tic disorder

616.83
MOE   Moe, Barbara

        Coping with Tourette
    syndrome and tic disorder

Coping with

TOURETTE SYNDROME AND TIC DISORDERS

Barbara Moe

The Rosen Publishing Group, Inc.
New York

This book is dedicated to the courageous young people who cope with tic disorders, Tourette syndrome, and associated conditions, and to the parents who encourage them.

Published in 2000, 2004 by The Rosen Publishing Group, Inc.
29 East 21st Street, New York, NY 10010

Revised Edition 2004

Library of Congress Cataloging-in-Publication Data
Moe, Barbara
Coping with Tourette Syndrome and tic disorders/by Barbara Moe.
     p. cm.—(Coping)
Includes bibliographical references and index.
Summary: Discusses the causes, manifestations, and ways to cope with Tourette Syndrome and other related tic disorders.
ISBN 0-8239-4089-6
1. Tourette Syndrome in adolescence—Juvenile literature.
2. Tourette Syndrome in children—Juvenile literature.
3. Attention-deficit disorder in adolescence—Juvenile literature. [1. Tourette Syndrome. 2. Tic disorders]
I. Title. II. Series.
RJ496.T68M64 1999
616.8'3—dc21
                                                    99-54519

Manufactured in the United States of America

Contents

All About Tourette Syndrome

In August, John, age sixteen, moved to a new city with his parents and fourteen-year-old sister. John had never taken medication for his tics, but he didn't want to start his junior year in a new school with kids making fun of him. So John and his family met with a neurologist at the adolescent clinic at Children's Hospital. Here's how that meeting began:

Dr. Shepherd: So what can I help you with today?

John's mom: I'm dreading the beginning of school. John can never get ready on time.

John: It's hard for me to get the right clothes picked out and do all the other things I have to do. I have to set my alarm for 5 AM.

John's dad: It's his obsessive-compulsive disorder. When he was in first grade, he had to arrange a hundred little cars—just so—before he'd leave his room in the morning. Sometimes his sister would tease him by pushing one car out of line, which drove him crazy.

John's mom: Of course, that wasn't the only problem. The tics started with blinking, then lip smacking and sniffing. In third grade he started making noises. He'd bark like a dog. His teacher thought he was doing it deliberately.

John: But I wasn't.

John's dad: John has always had learning problems. He's gotten special resource-room help. But he's a good kid. He tries really hard.

John: My last doctor said I had attention deficit hyperactivity disorder, and she put me on Ritalin. But it made my tics worse, so I quit taking it. My worst tic these days is the thought that I have to stretch my right leg way back. It hurts to do, and even worse, it's embarrassing.

John's dad: I had tics, too, when I was a kid.

Dr. Shepherd: Tourette syndrome and related disorders, such as ADHD, do tend to run in families. You all seem to have a good grasp of John's problems. Thanks for bringing his records. As you know, John has Tourette syndrome with motor and vocal tics. He also has problems common in those with tic disorders—attention difficulties, obsessions and compulsions, and learning problems. It's annoying. Right?

John: Right!

Dr. Shepherd: But help is available. Let's go for it.

John has understanding parents and a doctor who is experienced in treating people with Tourette syndrome. Both supports are useful when you're dealing with tic disorders and Tourette syndrome. John's case illustrates many of the features of this sometimes frustrating and constantly changing condition, which we will explore more fully in the discussion that follows.

What Are Tics? What Is Tourette Syndrome?

Tics are short, sudden, involuntary movements or sounds that seem to appear out of nowhere in a person who otherwise acts like everyone else. Tic disorders present themselves on a continuum from mild to severe. The most severe form of tic disorder is Tourette syndrome, sometimes called Gilles de la Tourette's syndrome.

Tourette syndrome (TS) is a neurological condition that involves involuntary muscle movements and uncontrollable vocal sounds. Both are called "tics." The word "syndrome" means a group of symptoms, and "tic" is a French word for "twitch."

Tics come and go—from one hour to the next, from one day to the next, and from one year to the next. They tend to come in clusters, or bouts. They wax and wane. Sometimes John has no tics at all; at other times, he has a lot. A tic disorder is different in each person.

Motor tics are sudden, purposeless, involuntary movements, such as eye blinking. (John doesn't blink because he has a piece of sand in his eye; he blinks because he "has to blink.") Vocal tics are involuntary sounds, such as throat clearing. (John doesn't have a piece of popcorn stuck in his throat, and he doesn't have a cold. He clears his throat because he has a compulsion to do so.)

Tics may be so mild that no one notices them, or they may be so severe that they disrupt a person's life and the lives of those around him or her. To be diagnosed with Tourette syndrome, a person must have tics that began in childhood and have at least two different motor tics and one or more verbal tics off and on for a period of at least one year. Tics sometimes disappear for weeks or months at a time, but when they come back, they may change in frequency, location, and type.

In addition to tics, other conditions are often part of the Tourette syndrome picture. Leslie Packer, Ph.D., calls Tourette syndrome with related conditions "TS plus." The most common associated conditions are (1) attention deficit disorder with or without hyperactivity (ADHD), (2) obsessive-compulsive disorder (OCD), (3) various kinds of learning difficulties (LD), (4) behavioral difficulties, and (5) sleep problems.

There is good news and not-as-good news for people with Tourette syndrome. The not-as-good news is that scientists have not yet discovered a cure for TS, and it can interfere with daily living. In some cases, it can continue off and on for a long time. The good news is that Tourette syndrome is never a life-threatening condition, and doctors can treat it. People can also learn to make changes in their lives so they can cope with it.

Who Gets Tic Disorders and Tourette Syndrome?

Males get Tourette syndrome more often than females. Many experts estimate that about 1 in every 100 boys and about 1 in every 600 girls get Tourette syndrome. Some experts say that as many as 1 in every 200 persons has or has had some type of tic disorder. People all over the world get tic disorders and Tourette syndrome. In the United States, Tourette syndrome seems to occur most frequently in Caucasians. In the past, tic disorders and Tourette syndrome were underdiagnosed because doctors and members of the general public didn't know as much about this condition as they do now.

Geneticists (people who study how traits are inherited) believe TS is inherited. A dominant gene (or genes) might cause different symptoms in different family members. In other words, if you have Tourette syndrome, chances are that one of your relatives had some form of this condition. Your relative's symptoms may have been so mild that no one even noticed them. You may find this knowledge comforting. For example, "My dad had Tourette syndrome, and he turned out great." On the other hand, you might find it frustrating to consider that your mom had tics, but that your tic disorder is worse than hers ever was.

What Are Some Risk Factors for Tourette Syndrome?

The major risk factor for Tourette syndrome is genetic. Often a parent or other close relative had tics in childhood. When both parents had tics and/or associated disorders such as OCD and ADHD, the risk increases for their children to have tics. Scientists have found genes on several different chromosomes that correlate with tics.

Possible nongenetic risk factors include low birth weight; maternal use of substances such as caffeine, alcohol, or cigarettes during pregnancy; maternal stress during pregnancy; and difficulties at the time of delivery.

Scientists believe that group A beta-hemolytic streptococcal infections in some individuals may cause the onset or a flare-up of tics or obsessive-compulsive disorder. PANDAS (pediatric autoimmune neuropsychiatric disorders associated with streptococcal infections) is the acronym for this susceptibility. In some people with Tourette syndrome, antibodies (proteins in the blood that fight the streptococcal bacteria) cross-react with areas in the brain that control movement. These antineuronal antibodies, which work against a normal body structure (brain cells or neurons), are called autoimmune ("against self") antibodies.

Those affected may have an abrupt and dramatic increase in tics or, more often, obsessive-compulsive symptoms. Sometimes other motor symptoms, such as jerky movements, or behavior problems, such as anxiety, also appear.

In rare cases, an affected person might benefit from the prevention of streptococcal infections. The doctor could prescribe a long-acting penicillin injection once a month. An experimental treatment that has helped some patients is intravenous immunoglobulin given at the time of the flare-up. However, the symptoms of most people with Tourette syndrome do not have a clear-cut association with streptococcal infections. Research is ongoing.

When Do People Get Tourette Syndrome? How Long Does It Last?

Tourette syndrome is a condition that begins in childhood—in other words, before age twenty-one. (Some experts say before the age of eighteen.) Most often, TS appears between the ages of two and fifteen, even if people don't recognize it at the time. Age seven is the most common age of onset. Sometimes when people's allergies flare up, their tics seem to get worse.

In about one-third of the cases, tics gradually disappear by the late teens; in another third, the symptoms decrease greatly. In the last third of the cases, tics continue into adulthood. It is common for Tourette syndrome to begin in childhood, to get worse before puberty, to get somewhat better in adolescence, and to stabilize in adulthood.

Doctors have no way of predicting which situations will suddenly improve and which ones won't. This is part of the frustration of TS. It is unlike other afflictions. If you have a severe case of acne, you can assure yourself that the condition will probably disappear after adolescence. With Tourette syndrome, you're never certain whether the tics are gone for good or whether they're going to reappear, possibly in some other form.

Treating Tourette Syndrome with Medication

Medication helps to control tics for some people but does not work for everyone. There is no way of knowing ahead of time what will work for whom or if a certain medication will help at all.

Dopamine-receptor blocking agents (neuroleptics) are the most tested and effective medications for tics. (Dopamine is a neurotransmitter; many authorities believe that faulty neurotransmission plays an important role in causing Tourette syndrome.) The Food and Drug Administration (FDA) has approved two neuroleptics to reduce tics: pimozide (Orap) and haloperidol (Haldol). Doctors usually increase the dosages of these drugs slowly, prescribing them for bedtime at first and later (if necessary) in divided doses twice a day. Side effects may include drowsiness, weight gain, and slow or foggy thinking. Newer ("atypical") neuroleptics include risperidone (Risperdal) and olanzapine (Zyprexa). All of the neuroleptic drugs can have the very rare side effects of excessively restless movements, dystonic spasms, or rigidity (stiffness).

Another class of medications used to treat tics (and ADHD) are the alpha-2 adrenergic agonists. Examples

11

are clonidine (Catapres) and guanfacine (Tenex). These medications require a single bedtime dose at first. If necessary, the doctor can increase the dosage to three times a day. Possible side effects include low blood pressure, headaches, and drowsiness. Clonidine is also available in transdermal patches with anti-tic effects lasting five to seven days.

Other possible agents for the treatment of tics are clonazepam (Klonopin); pergolide mesylate (Permax); baclofen (Lioresal), a muscle relaxant; cannabinoids (marijuana); and nicotine gum or patches.

For patients with extremely severe tics, doctors might use different treatments. For example, intramuscular botulinum toxin has been used for severe muscle-spasm tics. Experimentally, the use of intravenous immune globulin may cause a reduction in severe obsessive-compulsive (and tic) flare-ups.

However, drugs used to treat conditions associated with Tourette syndrome and tic disorders may turn out to have a more important role than the tic medications themselves.

A Short History of Tourette Syndrome

Evidence shows that about two thousand years ago, Aretaeus of Cappadocia recorded instances in which perfectly sane people twitched, grimaced, swore, and barked. Some say the Roman emperor Claudius had symptoms of Tourette syndrome. But recognition of such cases, which might have been Tourette syndrome, lagged until 1825. That year a French physician, Dr. Jean-Mare Itard, reported that his patient, a French noblewoman, had strange body movements and made barking sounds. Without meaning

12

Frequently Asked Questions About Tic Disorders and Tourette Syndrome

Question: Aren't tics just bad habits that people could control if they really wanted to?

Answer: Sometimes people can stop their tics for a short time, but eventually such control becomes impossible and the tics reappear. Young people who succeed at controlling their tics at school sometimes have to "let go" at home. Like trying to hold back from scratching an itch that must be scratched, holding back a tic can be so distracting that the person can focus only on restraint. Tics often decrease when people are relaxing or concentrating on something that intrigues them, but tics tend to increase with anxiety and stress.

Question: Can a person catch Tourette syndrome?
Answer: No. TS is not contagious.

Question: Does Tourette syndrome cause a low IQ?
Answer: No. Most people with Tourette syndrome have average or above average intelligence. Many people with Tourette syndrome are extremely creative. Some have learning disabilities, which will be discussed later.

Question: Does Tourette syndrome cause physical or mental deterioration?
Answer: No. TS does not cause intellectual or physical deterioration, and those with Tourette syndrome can expect to live as long and as well as anyone.

Question: I know a guy with Tourette syndrome, and he acts crazy. Does he have psychological problems?

Answer: Psychological problems are not the cause of tics. Tic disorders and Tourette syndrome are based on a person's heredity. People with tics and TS face special challenges. They must not only cope with TS but also with the social stigma (negative reactions and teasing from others) that accompanies it. This social stigma may lower a person's self-esteem. In some cases, a person's positive responses to the negative reactions of others may make him or her more psychologically healthy than someone who has never faced such difficulties.

Question: I have a friend who has TS, and he's a wild man. I don't mean the tics. He's as funny as a stand-up comedian. He makes people laugh.
Answer: Some people with Tourette syndrome have quirky personalities that amuse their friends. No one knows if the clown in a certain person is (1) his or her personality, (2) part of TS, or (3) a way of trying to cover up the condition.

Question: Do people with tics have to take medication?
Answer: Most people, especially those with mild tics, do not need to take medication.

Question: What if I'm a person who needs medication? Am I going to need it forever?
Answer: In some people, tics increase in the teen years; in others, tics decrease in the late teens. If you decide you're tired of taking pills and want to stop, tell your doctor. Never just stop cold. In quitting any medication, it's best to taper off. Otherwise, you can get a rebound effect, or a worsening of symptoms. The other important thing to remember is that medication can't help if you don't take it. Derek's mom says,

"Derek takes his pills for a while and starts feeling better. Then he decides he doesn't need medication anymore. That's when he begins to have problems."

Question: Are there any strategies to reduce tics without medication?

Answer: Some doctors have recommended behavioral treatments to try to reduce the frequency of tics. These techniques include relaxation, self-monitoring, and habit-reversal training (HRT). Relaxation techniques, such as abdominal breathing and progressive muscle relaxation, which are discussed in chapter 5, relieve tics in some people. Others benefit from self-monitoring in which the person with TS counts each tic in an effort to reduce frequency. HRT focuses on learning a response that is opposite of the tic. (Why this training uses the word "habit" when tics are not habits may relate to the fact that some people used to call tics "habit spasms.") Use of HRT for a motor tic might involve tensing a muscle to try to prevent a tic. To try to prevent a vocal tic, the person might try deep breathing through the nose with the mouth closed.

Question: Do allergies cause tics?

Answer: No. Seasonal allergies seem to make tics worse, as do allergy medications in some people. At times, viral infections also seem to increase tics for a short time.

Question: Could you describe a typical case of Tourette syndrome?

Answer: There is no typical case of Tourette syndrome. Each person's condition is different.

to, she also blurted out obscene words (a condition called coprolalia). Because of her tics, she lived in isolation for most of her life. Experts say Itard's report is probably the first known description of Tourette syndrome.

Sixty years later, Georges Gilles de la Tourette, another French physician, referred to Itard's patient and reviewed eight similar cases. These persons had tics, coprolalia, and echolalia (the repetition of the last-heard sound).

In those days, many people thought of Tourette syndrome as a rare condition caused by psychological problems. These days we realize tic disorders and TS are relatively common. The cause is genetic, not emotional.

Well-Known People with Tourette Syndrome

Many famous people seem to have had, or were suspected of having, Tourette syndrome—even before anyone knew what it was!

Samuel Johnson, writer, critic, and judge, was born in England and lived from 1709 to 1784. Those who knew him observed the "convulsive movements" of his hands, lips, feet, and knees, but no one at that time knew of Tourette syndrome. As a young man, Johnson was passed over for a job as an assistant headmaster at a boys' school because of his facial grimaces. His friend, James Boswell, author of the famous biography *The Life of Samuel Johnson*, explains why Johnson didn't last long as head of his own school. "He did not appear to have been profoundly revered by his pupils. His oddities of manner, and uncouth gesticulations, could not but be the subject of merriment to them." Then, as well as now, people with

Tourette syndrome faced prejudice. Nevertheless, this interesting man, with his friend, the painter Joshua Reynolds, organized the London Literary Club. Johnson wielded tremendous influence over the society of his day.

Some people have speculated that the musical genius Wolfgang Amadeus Mozart (1756–1791) had Tourette syndrome. The book *The Letters of Mozart*, edited by Emily Anderson, gives some examples of Mozart's word games, rhyming words, and repetitions. Because this type of writing shows up mostly in Mozart's letters to his female cousins rather than letters to his father, one might assume that Mozart was merely trying to impress. Here is an example:

> *Today the letter setter from my Papa Ha Ha! Dropped safely into my claws paws. I hope that you too have got shot the note dote, which I wrote to you from Manheim. If so, so much the better, better the much so. Now for some sense. I am very sorry to hear that the Abbott rabbit has had another stroke so soon moon.*
>
> —Mozart, letter to a friend

Nearly 125 years ago, Leo Tolstoy wrote the famous novel *Anna Karenina*. One of the book's characters is Nikolai Levin. Evidence suggests that Tolstoy patterned the character Nikolai after his own brother, Dmitry. Tolstoy describes Nikolai as having motor tics (twitching eyebrows, neck stretching, head and body jerks) and also vocal tics such as "flinging insults" at people.

You've probably never heard of Witty Ticcy Ray. Most people haven't. Ray cannot be considered to be a well-known person with Tourette syndrome. But if you read his story in Oliver Sacks's 1985 book, *The Man Who Mistook His Wife for a Hat,* you may feel as if you do know this excellent drummer and table-tennis player, who also became a husband and father. In a later book, *An Anthropologist on Mars,* Sacks writes about a surgeon with Tourette syndrome and claims to know four other surgeons with this condition.

Many famous people have Tourette syndrome and aren't embarrassed to talk about it. Their sharing helps others. One of these people was professional basketball player Mahmoud Abdul-Rauf. Actually, some people attribute his ability to concentrate during a difficult play to Tourette syndrome. As a basketball star at Louisiana State University, before he converted to the Islamic faith, Chris Jackson (his given name) scored fifty-five points in a single game.

Another outstanding athlete and spokesperson for TS is major league baseball player Jim Eisenreich. In 1996, he established a foundation in his own name for children with Tourette syndrome. Now married and a father, Eisenreich looks back on problems he had in elementary school. He had trouble sitting still for more than a couple minutes and had tics that some considered the result of psychiatric illness. Today, many people don't understand tic disorders and TS, but the situation was even worse twenty years ago. In spite of his tics, Eisenreich played Little League baseball. After playing baseball at St. Cloud University, he started with the Minnesota Twins and went on to play for the Kansas City Royals, the Philadelphia Phillies, and the Florida Marlins.

Tourette syndrome involves tics, but it is not merely a tic disorder. Tourette syndrome is a complex condition affecting many areas of a person's life, including relationships with himself or herself, family, and friends, as well as in school, work, and life in general.

Classifications of Tic Disorders and Tourette Syndrome

One job of doctors is to classify tic disorders. The following categories explain how tic disorders exist on a scale from mild to severe.

There are various ways to classify tics, but experts usually divide them into two main groups: motor (involving muscle movements) and vocal (involving speech). Of course, technically speaking, speech requires the use of muscles, but we need not be that technical. Each of the two main categories has two sub-categories: simple and complex.

Motor Tics

Simple Motor Tics
Simple motor tics usually involve one muscle group. The first symptom that often shows up is a rapid muscle spasm in a small area of the face around the eyes or mouth. Some experts say that 20 to 25 percent of children have these simple tics at one time or another. After a short time, they may disappear, never to return. Examples are blinking, squinting, or rolling the eyes; smacking or licking the lips; or sticking out the tongue.

Complex Motor Tics

Complex motor tics might involve a series of simple tics or more complicated movements. Most often, these tics start in the upper body and move down. To those watching, it seems as if the person is making purposeful movements when he or she actually is not. Examples are bending over, pinching, poking, kicking, jumping, touching, snapping the fingers, stamping the feet, and pulling on clothing. Some people actually hurt themselves without meaning to. For example, Tom rubs his index finger over his thumb so many times a day that his finger gets blistered. The following are rare motor tics.

- Echopraxia or echokinesis: imitation of another person's movements

- Copropraxia: obscene gestures

Jane, sixteen, says, "There was this kid in my sixth-grade class who used to go around giving everybody the finger. He even did this to teachers, but other than that, he was a nice kid. Some people thought he was going crazy. But now we know it was really a tic."

Vocal Tics

Simple Vocal Tics

Simple vocal tics are also called verbal or phonic tics or verbalizations. Young people often have motor tics for some time before other people begin noticing they are making noises that seem to be out of their control. The person may be able to soften the sound or disguise it in some way. Throat clearing and grunting are the most common vocal tics. Examples of other vocal tics are coughing, burping, hiccuping, barking, sniffing, and snorting.

Complex Vocal Tics

In some instances, the sound a person makes turns into syllables, words, phrases, or even sentences. Some sounds people make get very loud, even becoming explosive. In rare cases, the sound becomes an obscenity or cussword. Sometimes the person is able to change the bad word or phrase so that it sounds acceptable. For example, "up yours" might become "oh, sores." The following are rare vocal tics.

➥ Echolalia is repeating the last word or phrase of another person. For example, if a teacher says, "Please stay at your desk," Jack may say "desk" or "at your desk."

➥ Palilalia is repeating one's own last word. For example, Bill might say, "I have to go now, now, now."

➥ Coprolalia is swearing without meaning to.

Researchers estimate that only 10 to 15 percent of those with Tourette syndrome have coprolalia. Experts used to consider coprolalia to be a hallmark of Tourette syndrome. This misunderstanding deserves correction.

Other Tic Disorders

Experts also classify tic disorders by when they begin, how long they last, and how severe they are.

Transient Tic Disorder

Transient tic disorder (TTD) is a condition involving single or multiple motor tics that last less than one year. The word "transient" means "passing." Often the person has only one tic and the doctor does not prescribe medical treatment.

> Sam is only four years old. When he was two, his parents adopted him from an orphanage in Russia. Over the past three months, Sam's parents have noticed that when their son concentrates on a task, such as drawing, he repeatedly blinks his eyes and squints. The blinking frustrates Sam, and he tries to stop it by rubbing his eyes. Sometimes he also jerks his head. Sam's doctor says Sam has transient tics of childhood.

Chronic Tic Disorder

Chronic tic disorder (CTD) involves motor or vocal tics (but not both) lasting longer than one year. Doctors do not usually prescribe medication for this condition either, especially if the person has only a simple motor tic. Experts believe that CTD is a mild form of Tourette syndrome and, like TS, may be inherited.

> Keisha has several tics. Two years ago at Christmastime, her mother noticed excessive blinking. Keisha also shrugs her shoulders and sometimes throws her head back so hard that she cries out in pain. At other times,

she yawns repeatedly and scrunches up her nose like a rabbit. Doctors have diagnosed Keisha's condition as chronic tic disorder. At this time, Keisha's parents are not interested in putting her on medication.

Tourette Syndrome

Tourette syndrome is the most serious tic disorder. TS involves motor tics and at least one vocal tic. Tourette syndrome begins in childhood (before age twenty-one) and lasts longer than one year. Tics may include almost any body movement or sound imaginable.

Greg's mother first noticed his blinking when he was two or three years old. Now when people focus attention on him, such as when he's standing in front of the class giving a report, he may hop on one foot. Sometimes he shakes both hands at his sides. Several times in a museum or department store, Greg has swung his arms around in wide circles. If he's singing with a group, he may sway from side to side, not necessarily in time to the music. Up to now, Greg has had one verbal tic, which could be a habit; he clears his throat frequently. Recently, however, he has begun to shout four-letter words, "shut up," and other words people don't expect to hear in polite conversation. This is embarrassing to him and to his parents. Because of the bad words, Greg's mom made an appointment with the doctor.

Greg's doctor did not diagnose Tourette syndrome, not yet anyway, because Greg's verbal tics have not persisted for a year. However, he plans to stay in touch

24

with Greg and his family. Later on, if symptoms persist, the doctor may classify Greg's symptoms as Tourette syndrome. Medication may have a role now or later.

Dystonic Tics

Most tics are quick and sudden, but occasionally a tic can be a slow movement. These movements, such as the writhing or twisting of the body, are called dystonic tics. For example, in our beginning story, John has the feeling he needs to stretch his right leg way back and hold it there. Most experts would call this action and the sustaining of this unusual position a dystonic tic.

Sensory Tics

Sensory tics are not really tics but sensations that (in some people) precede the tic. For example, Sam (mentioned earlier) has simple motor tics. But he also complains of a pain that "feels like an earache" in his eye before the tic occurs. Most doctors would call this a sensory tic.

Some young people (approximately 40 percent of those with Tourette syndrome) describe feelings of pressure, tickling, warmth, or cold in their bones, joints, muscles, or on their skin. To relieve the feeling, they make a quick movement (a tic). Other people make noises in response to sensory stimulation in their throats or voice boxes.

Impossible to Classify?

There is much about Tourette syndrome that defies classification. TS is frustrating but also fascinating. We can compare Tourette syndrome to a computer screen that seems to have links to almost everything. David E. Comings's book, *Tourette Syndrome and Human Behavior*, contains 828 pages linking TS to many other conditions—from alcoholism to eating disorders, from compulsive gambling to panic attacks. In the introduction to the book *Don't Think About Monkeys*, coeditor John Hilkevich reminds us that he has Tourette syndrome. However, if he were asked to see another person with TS, he "would still not know what to expect, as its symptoms are so diverse, so integrated into the personality, so complex, so multifaceted." The fact is that, as yet, we don't know enough about Tourette syndrome. Researchers have much more work to do.

Classification of tic disorders helps in a discussion of Tourette syndrome, but we also must consider associated conditions, which we will do in the chapters that follow.

Related Disorders

Now that we've classified tic disorders, let's take a look at other problems that may be part of the bigger Tourette syndrome picture.

> *Megan, age fifteen, says, "Sometimes my tics tick me off. But the worst part for me, especially when I was younger, was having to go to about fifty different doctors. First, to the ophthalmologist to see if there was something wrong with my eyes because of the blinking. Then, there was the allergist because of my coughing. Now I have to go to the social worker at school and to the psychologist after school for my ADHD and OCD. Also, I attend a socialization group to learn how to get along with people better. And then there's my neurologist who monitors my meds. I don't have much time left for fun."*

As mentioned earlier, a variety of other conditions can accompany tic disorders and Tourette syndrome. Sometimes authorities collect all of the associated conditions under an umbrella term: Tourette syndrome spectrum disorder. A person might have one or more of these problems, but fortunately hardly anyone has all of them. The most common related conditions include attention disorders, sometimes called ADs and also diagnosed as attention deficit hyperactivity disorder (ADHD); obsessions and compulsions, sometimes diagnosed as obsessive-compulsive disorder (OCD); learning disorders or differences (LD); behavioral problems; and sleep disorders.

Attention Deficit Hyperactivity Disorder

Attention deficits can occur as part of Tourette syndrome or they can stand alone. Attention deficit disorder (ADD) and attention deficit hyperactivity disorder (ADHD) describe conditions in which a person has trouble paying attention and acts impulsively. Consider the following types of attention deficits.

⮑ Mostly inattentive

⮑ Predominantly hyperactive and impulsive

⮑ A combination of these two types

According to many experts, approximately 80 percent of boys and about 50 percent of girls with attention disorders are also hyperactive. They are restless, in a hurry, and constantly on the go. A recent supplement to the *Journal of the Academy of Child and Adolescent Psychiatry* says that 65 percent of people who were hyperactive as children continue to have some symptoms as adults. About half of the young people who have ADHD also have a learning disability even though they are of normal intelligence.

Doctors believe that the following statements about attention deficits are true.

- ➷ Attention deficits are often inherited. In many cases, the person with ADHD has a relative with the same condition.

- ➷ Attention deficits can show up years before the symptoms of TS appear.

- ➷ Attention deficits are not limited to inattention, although inattentive behavior and difficulty concentrating are usually part of the picture.

Most people have trouble concentrating at times, especially if they're not interested in a particular subject. All of us feel irritable sometimes and have trouble settling down. We all do impulsive things, such as acting before thinking. Who has never been angry and exploded? We can all remember occasions when we wish we had kept our mouths shut. But people with ADHD have these troubles (and more) most of the time.

Scott was the youngest of three boys. Born two weeks early, he weighed just a little more than five pounds. He walked later and talked later than his older brothers. Mom, busy with the other two boys, was less than patient when Scott climbed into the kitchen sink to get what he wanted out of the cupboard. (He didn't think to ask; besides, that would have taken too long.) He hit other kids

29

instead of talking out disagreements. Scott was somewhat clumsy, too; he always seemed to be falling over his feet. At age four, he managed to knock out his two upper front teeth.

In first grade, Scott started blinking as if he had something in his eyes. At first, his parents thought he had an eye infection. He was nearsighted and had to wear glasses. When he scrunched up his nose, his parents thought he was trying to keep his glasses from falling off his face. He said his nose itched. Sometimes he made doglike barking or growling noises. To go along with the noises, he crawled on the floor and bit people's shoestrings.

When Scott didn't learn to read in first grade, his parents became worried and had him tested. The tester noted that Scott wanted to learn and valued his academic achievements. However, he rushed through easy tasks and avoided difficult ones. When frustrated by anything, he whined or got angry. His body moved almost constantly. The tester wrote: "He is distractible and inattentive and resists looking at the person talking to him. In communication with others, Scott often rambles and rarely waits for (and rarely seems to expect) a response. When others are talking to him, Scott is usually looking elsewhere or doing something else. His work and work area are sloppy, partly because of fine motor problems and partly because of hurrying. His writing has a shaky quality, and he has trouble using scissors."

One doctor suggested medication for the tics (no one ever mentioned ADHD), but Scott's mother didn't like the idea of drugs. She gave him herbs instead.

Another doctor suggested a special school for kids with learning difficulties, but Scott vetoed that idea. He wanted to go to the same public school his brothers had attended. In high school, although he barely made the soccer team and rarely got to play, he managed to be on the varsity team as a senior.

Scott is now twenty-three years old. He's in good shape from working out every day at the recreation center, where he has many friends. He doesn't miss participating in competitive sports. After five years of college, he was certified as a first-grade teacher. The kids love him. But Scott doesn't date (probably because of his low self-esteem) and dislikes talking about his feelings.

His mother often asks herself: "What if? What if Scott had taken medication for ADHD? What if they could have persuaded him to go to a special school for his learning disabilities? What if he'd attended a therapy group? What if we had participated in family therapy?"

What if? What if? What if? Actually, Scott's mom is proud of her son for the good person he has turned out to be and for everything he has accomplished in spite of his difficulties.

Accurate reporting of symptoms helps in making the correct diagnosis of ADHD. Sometimes after the doctor prescribes medication, the person experiences dramatic results.

Maria, age seventeen, says, "I've had tics and ADHD since preschool. I didn't want to take any medications. I didn't want to be different. What I didn't think of was that my tics and ADHD already made me different. My parents and doctor talked me into a trial period with Ritalin. I joked about my 'drug' to my friends. But I gave it a chance. For me it was like what a blind person must feel on regaining sight. For once I could concentrate and get organized."

Tourette syndrome presents a special challenge to the doctor and to the patient. Working together, they must figure out which of the associated symptoms to treat. Sometimes treatment for one problem makes another problem worse. For example, stimulant medication, such as Ritalin (methylphenidate) or Adderall (mixed amphetamines) for ADHD, can occasionally worsen tics. A similar medication is Concerta (long-acting methylphenidate).

How Common Are Attention Disorders?

Because making an accurate diagnosis of ADHD is not always easy, experts can only guess at its prevalence. Recent estimates suggest that at least 3 to 5 percent (2 million) young people in the United States have ADHD. Some say that approximately 10 percent of boys and 5 percent of girls have this condition.

Attention disorders are the most common behavior problem of young people in the United States. But young people from other countries also have ADHD. Experts know a lot about ADHD, but there is still much they don't know, especially about the condition in adolescents and young adults.

Researchers are giving more attention to attention disorders, but doctors in past years saw people with these disorders, too. In the recent past, doctors used such terms as "cerebral dysfunction," "brain-injured child," or "minimal brain dysfunction" to describe ADHD. Some put emphasis on the excessive activity, using terms such as "hyperkinetic behavior syndrome," "hyperkinetic impulse disorder," or "hyperactive child syndrome."

ADHD is confusing, but when combined with Tourette syndrome, the picture can become even more confusing. For example, 50 to 60 percent of people with Tourette syndrome have attention disorders, while 10 percent of those with ADHD have tics.

But that is only the beginning of possible confusion. Just as there is no X ray or blood test to diagnose Tourette syndrome, there is likewise no commonly used definitive test for ADHD. Doctors must rely on reports from parents, teachers, and young people themselves to help make a diagnosis. Even with the best reporting, it can be next to impossible to figure out which behavior comes from which condition. For example, people with Tourette syndrome sometimes have behavior problems. But then, so do people with ADHD.

Sometimes, using their best judgment, doctors prescribe medication for young people who don't need medication. On the other hand, many young people with ADHD are never diagnosed. They miss receiving medications that could help them. Some parents are eager to have their children try pills to "fix" them. Other parents are suspicious of all medications. (These parents are at opposite ends of the issue. Sometimes a middle ground is best.)

Behavior Problems Associated with ADHD

The most common behavioral problems associated with ADHD fall into three main categories: problems with impulses, attention, and activity.

Problems with Impulses

The word "impulsive" means acting before thinking of the consequences of one's actions. Young children's impulsive behaviors are different from those of teenagers. In our earlier story, Scott (in his younger days) pushed ahead of others in line. He hurried through his math problems to finish first—even if half of his answers were wrong. He didn't finish listening to the directions of parents and teachers before doing what he wanted to do. He got into fights and hit other kids. He tried to settle arguments with his fists. Afterward, he felt bad about his impulsive behaviors.

Fortunately, as he grew older, Scott learned ways to control his impulses. Until he learned impulse control, his parents refused to let him drive a car. Teens who haven't learned impulse control can be a danger to themselves and others.

Problems with Attention

People with ADHD have a hard time paying attention. They can concentrate, but concentration for them takes intense effort. Parents and teachers might need to look children straight in the eyes when asking them to do something. Or they may need to give the child one direction at a time instead of a series of directions. As young people grow older, they might want to tell their parents they are not deliberately showing disrespect.

34

A person with ADHD can also become easily distracted. The person might start working with great interest on a project only to abandon the project five minutes later. All sorts of things can act as distractions—people talking or moving in the same room, flickering lights, even a person's own thoughts.

Problems with Activity

To say people are hyperactive or "hyper" means that they are excessively active. In Scott's case, hyperactivity meant he moved even when he sat in a chair. For young children, hyperactivity might mean flitting from one activity to another. As people grow older, they learn to control their movements, but their thoughts might be in turmoil; they might feel restless or irritable. Matt said, "My nerve endings feel raw. I feel like chalk grating on a blackboard. I feel like I have carbonated water in my blood vessels." Some people show hyperactivity in their speech. They seem to talk all the time and don't stop to listen. They interrupt or butt into other people's conversations.

Effects of These Problems

The basic problem with all these symptoms is that the individual who has them often feels disorganized or out of control. It seems as if that person's brain wires are twisted or frayed—sending sparks flying in all directions. The part of the person's brain responsible for organizing and/or inhibiting actions isn't working efficiently. To outsiders it seems as if the person is acting deliberately. Instead, a defect in the brain is causing the trouble, not the person himself or herself.

The good news is that many of the symptoms of ADHD get better as a person gets older. Recognition and treatment of these conditions improve the quality of life for people with attention disorders. The sad part is that, in some cases, ADHD is not recognized or treated. As a result, some people grow up with feelings of failure; low self-esteem; strained relationships with parents, teachers, and friends; and general confusion about their place in the world.

Medical Treatment of ADHD

Treatment of ADHD is sometimes as complicated as the disorder itself, especially when ADHD "partners" with Tourette syndrome. Knowing the following two facts will increase positive outcomes: (1) If the doctor, psychologist, school personnel, family members, and the person with the disorder all work together, the result will be better than without this cooperation. (2) A standard treatment for all people is likely to be ineffective. Each person's disorder is unique, and therefore, each individual's treatment needs to be tailored to that person's needs. We'll discuss nonmedical treatment and coping techniques in a later chapter. For now, we'll go over some of the medications that may be helpful.

Not all people with ADHD need medication, but many do. When doctors talk about medication for ADHD, they most often mean stimulant medication, such as Ritalin. Stimulants for a person who is hyper? Does that make sense? For many people it does. For those with ADHD, stimulants in correct dosages can cause better organization; the person can concentrate and have more stable moods.

Almost everyone has heard stories about Ritalin abuse: people in high school selling it to friends or college students taking it to stay up all night to cram for a test. Ritalin and other stimulant medications used for ADHD, such as Dexadrine (dextroamphetamine), Cylert (pemoline), and Adderall (mixed amphetamines), are sometimes called "speed"; people can abuse them.

No medication comes without potential side effects. The possible effects of Ritalin are tiredness, nervousness, and decreased appetite. Some young people have heard that Ritalin will stunt their growth, but most experts consider this concern groundless. Besides, a person can avoid this possible side effect by not taking the medication for at least four weeks out of the year, such as during the summer.

In about a third of those who have Tourette syndrome as well as ADHD, the stimulant medication can backfire and cause the TS symptoms to get worse. Why? Because stimulants increase the effects of certain brain chemicals such as dopamine and norepinephrine. People with Tourette syndrome may already have too much dopamine in certain brain areas. Often doctors prefer trying alternative medications.

In the past as an alternative to stimulants (or in combination with them), doctors sometimes prescribed the medications called tricyclic antidepressants (TSAs). These drugs can lessen the symptoms of ADHD without making tics worse. Examples are Norpramin (desipramine), Elavil (amitryptyline), Pamelor (nortriptyline), and Tofranil (imipramine). Possible side effects of this group of medications include sleep problems, dry mouth, constipation, and dizziness when standing up (postural hypotension).

Another group of antidepressants, called selective serotonin reuptake inhibitors (SSRIs), increase the levels of the neurotransmitter serotonin by preventing its "reuptake" by the nerve cells. Some of the most common SSRIs are

Prozac (fluoxetine), Zoloft (sertraline), Paxil (paroxetine), and Luvox (fluvoxamine). Side effects of these medications can include nausea, diarrhea or constipation, insomnia or fatigue, anxiety, and headaches. When using these drugs, some people report sexual problems—a major reason they want to discontinue the medication. Be sure to ask your doctor for advice. He or she might be able to reduce the dose or prescribe a different medication.

A word of caution: No medication by itself will "cure" ADHD, but the condition can be managed or controlled. Medications can relieve troublesome symptoms. But the positive effects of any one drug may not last forever, and a person might need to try others.

Obsessions and Compulsions

Obsessions are recurring thoughts, images, and impulses that are hard to shake off. They often involve a feeling that something bad is going to happen. Common obsessive thoughts focus on germs and dirt. Compulsions are behaviors done in response to those thoughts. Common compulsive behaviors are washing parts of the body repeatedly and touching or arranging things. If the obsessions and compulsions are severe and interfere with a person's life, doctors might describe the condition as obsessive-compulsive disorder (OCD). Some people have distressing obsessions without compulsions, but many people with TS have obsessive-compulsive disorder.

Experts sometimes divide OCD into two categories. The anxiety subtype involves worrying that something bad is about to happen. The person with this type of OCD relieves the anxiety by compulsions designed to decrease risk. For example, frequent hand-washing or toothbrushing might kill deadly germs. Checking rituals (such as checking the stove burners before leaving the house) might keep the house from burning down—in a person's mind.

The other OCD subtype involves getting things just right. The story of John in chapter 1 shows the "just right" type of OCD. People with Tourette syndrome more often have this subtype. Their obsessions and compulsions have to do with a feeling of incompleteness that is temporarily relieved when they do something "just right." In our first story, John is late for school every day because he has to keep trying on different clothes until he finds some that feel right.

Treatment can involve both counseling and medication. Specific medications may allow people who have obsessions and compulsions to concentrate on things they need to do, such as homework, rather than on their obsessive thoughts and compulsive behaviors. To provide this relief, doctors may prescribe medications from the selective serotonin reuptake inhibitors (SSRIs), sometimes called serotonin reuptake inhibitors (SRIs). Although these medications are most often used as antidepressants, doctors have found them useful in treating obsessive and compulsive symptoms.

An older drug, Anafranil (clomipramine), a tricyclic antidepressant, can help to reduce obsessive and compulsive symptoms in some people.

Learning Disorders

Experts estimate that up to 60 percent of young people with Tourette syndrome have learning problems. What kind of learning problems? The range is wide. As with

ADHD, learning problems might show up years before the tics start. Tourette syndrome and/or ADHD can affect any or all of the seven core areas of learning: oral expression, written expression, listening comprehension, reading comprehension, basic reading skills, mathematical reasoning, and math calculation.

Tics can disrupt the learning process of the people who have them. Sometimes, they also interfere with the concentration of classmates, who avoid those with tics even more and make them feel depressed. Tics can interfere with handwriting and participation in class discussion.

To make matters even more complicated, it is difficult (if not impossible) to sort out the contribution of coexisting conditions such as ADHD or OCD from learning problems.

Medication can help to control tics, but side effects of the drugs can affect learning. Ben's story illustrates how complicated the whole picture can become.

Ben has motor and vocal tics. So far, no medications (and he has tried a lot) have been able to stop his tics completely. For a couple of months, he has been sticking out his lower jaw and tensing his neck muscles so tightly that his neck tendons stick out. Sometimes he has to stop in the middle of whatever he's doing or saying to do this tic. At other times, he turns his head from side to side. When two kids at school asked him why he did this, Ben said his neck hurt. Ben grunts and clears his throat and sometimes makes strange noises by forcing air out of his mouth. Once when a classmate teased him, Ben put his hands around his classmate's neck as if he were about to choke him.

For a while, the drug Haldol helped Ben's tics. But on the high doses needed, Ben had troubling side effects.

Orap (pimozide) worked for a while, but eventually Ben's body built up a tolerance to the medication and his tics became worse. At the time Ben stopped the medication, his tics were so severe that, according to his dad, "He wriggled on the bed like a wounded snake." Recently Ben and his doctor have decided to give Tenex (guanfacine) a try.

At school for the past three years, Ben has had an IEP (individualized education plan), which allows him to receive special services. Ben has difficulty with auditory processing and following through with what he hears. Speech therapy is helping him to understand his teachers' directions better. In reading, Ben is about a year behind; he gets extra help in understanding what he reads and with expressing himself in writing. He also meets once a week with the school psychologist to help improve his self-esteem.

If a person can get tics under control (sometimes medication is needed), nonmedical treatment can help with learning problems. Keep in mind that each person's Tourette syndrome is different, each person's school is different, each person's home is different, and each person is different. Therefore, no single list of suggestions will work for everyone.

Behavior Disorders

Behavior disorders sometimes become mixed together with learning disorders. A coexisting condition such as ADHD might contribute to behavior problems. The following are examples of behavior problems.

- Restlessness, impulsiveness, inability to concentrate
- Aggressiveness, hostility, quick temper, overreaction
- Negativity, withdrawal, depression, moodiness
- Showing off, seeking attention

The term "behavior disorder" implies actions that affect others. It is not hard to figure out that some of the behaviors will cause problems in school. The incident in which Ben tried to choke a classmate earned him a few days of in-school suspension. (Although he got a lot of work done in the vice principal's office, it wasn't much fun.)

Disruptive behaviors bother other people and can also affect the self-esteem of the person who acts them out (that is, the person with Tourette syndrome and ADHD).

Doctors sometimes use the term "oppositional defiant disorder" (ODD) to describe behavior that is disobedient, hostile, and defiant.

Sleep Disorders

Many people with Tourette syndrome report having sleep problems. These difficulties can include the following.

- Trouble getting to sleep
- Waking up early

- Nightmares

- Sleepwalking

- Sleep talking

- Restlessness at night

- Bed-wetting

With help from a doctor and family members, a person can find ways to manage and overcome these problems. Some problems, like bed-wetting, can go away on their own; others might require more strategies that can be developed in counseling.

Summary

Tourette syndrome is a complicated condition; it can involve many associated difficulties. Sometimes the best thing to do is to figure out which associated difficulty is causing the most problems and try to go after that one first. As we've noted, treatment for one symptom sometimes makes another symptom worse. (Ben found out that some of the side effects from the medications were worse than the symptom they were supposed to treat.) Tourette syndrome is a condition you can live with, but it might require good humor, patience, and flexibility.

Tourette Syndrome and Depression

You can do it. You can live a happy and fulfilling life with Tourette syndrome. Let's face it. TS is a complicated condition. It comes and goes, it can involve associated conditions, and it can be embarrassing. But it is not a fatal disease. You may or may not need medications. But you will certainly need education and support.

We've taken a brief look at Tourette syndrome and its co-occurring conditions. Now let's find ways people can cope with some of these problems. We can divide the coping strategies into two large categories: generalized and specific. Generalized strategies can help anyone with Tourette syndrome. (Specific tips will follow for those with tic disorders, ADHD, OCD, learning and behavior problems, and sleep problems.)

The following is a greatly abbreviated interview with Brian, age seventeen; his mother; and Dr. Garrett, a pediatric neurologist. (Keep in mind that the visit to the doctor was not Brian's idea but his mother's.) The story illustrates some of the factors the doctor takes into consideration when making (or not making) a diagnosis of Tourette syndrome.

Dr. Garrett: What can I do to help?

Brian's mom: I want to know if he has Tourette syndrome. I got some information from the Internet and I think he has it.

Brian hunches over his knees. His mother has a way of making him feel like a little kid.

Dr. Garrett: Can you describe the problem?

Brian straightens up and opens his mouth to speak.

Brian's mom: It's his behavior. We've had to send him to a special school out of state. I've heard Tourette syndrome causes behavior problems and learning problems.

Dr. Garrett clears his throat. (Throat clearing is a longtime habit of his. He doesn't have Tourette syndrome. At least he doesn't think so.)

Dr. Garrett: Have you had tics, Brian?

Brian's mom: He used to blink his eyes a lot. He doesn't do that much anymore.

Brian stares at the floor.

Brian's mom: Well, his dad used to be his Boy Scout leader, and he remembers Brian making strange noises under his breath.

Dr. Garrett begins looking forward to the time (a few minutes from now) when he will invite Brian's mother to go out in the hall, so he can talk to Brian alone.

Dr. Garrett: Brian, have you ever felt an urge to do something over and over again until you got it perfect?

Brian's mom: Yes! Yes, he has. His teacher told me he used to pass notes in school and write them over and over.

Brian: That's because I always thought of more to say.

Dr. Garrett: How about attention problems like troubles with concentration?

Brian's mom: He certainly has!

Dr. Garrett: Are there any other problems?

Brian's mom: He's been in a drug rehab program— for smoking pot—and now we've had to send him to this special school.

Dr. Garrett: How's that going, Brian?

Brian straightens up and looks Dr. Garrett in the eye.

Brian: Good.

Brian's mom: He still doesn't do all his work or hand his papers in on time.

Dr. Garrett: I'll tell you what. I think I'd like to interview Brian alone for a few minutes.

Brian's mom goes out.

Dr. Garrett: So, Brian, it appears that you like your school.

Brian: It's pretty fun. I get to meet with a counselor whenever I want to. We have only two grades—A and B. If you don't turn in your work, you don't get a grade until you finish it.

Dr. Garrett: That's an interesting concept. It sounds made for success. What else do you like about school?

Brian: Well, I'm playing soccer and even scoring a few goals.

Dr. Garrett: Excellent. Let's see. Can you tell me . . . How are you feeling on a scale of one to ten? Do you feel down or depressed?

Brian: I feel pretty good. About a six or a seven.

Dr. Garrett: Have you had any sleep problems?

Brian: I sleep like a baby.

Dr. Garrett: Can you tell me something about your tics? [For the next ten minutes, they discuss Brian's tics. After that, Dr. Garrett calls Brian's mother back in. He's surprised to find her right outside the door. She sits down.]

Brian's mom: Well?

Dr. Garrett: I don't believe Brian has Tourette syndrome.

Brian's mom: You mean you're not going to prescribe any medication?

Dr. Garrett: Not at this time.

Brian's mom: You're saying you don't think Tourette syndrome is the cause of his problems?

Dr. Garrett: You've read and heard about Tourette syndrome and associated disorders, or co-occurring conditions. Various difficulties may go along with Tourette syndrome, but TS doesn't cause them. Brian may have had transient, or passing, tics when he was younger, but he doesn't have Tourette syndrome. Furthermore, I believe he'll get along well in life. I think your family might benefit from some counseling together—family counseling. If you'd like a referral, I'd be glad to give you some names.

Keep up the good work, Brian. It's been nice seeing you. I'd like you to consider the advice I just gave your mom. Thank you both for coming in.

In Brian's story, we see a mother who cares very much about her son. Dr. Garrett believes Brian has only transient tics of childhood, not Tourette syndrome. But Brian has a self-esteem problem, which is common with tic disorders. Let's move on to some tips about self-esteem.

Self-Esteem: If You Don't Have It, You Can Still Get It!

High self-esteem (or what some people call a good self-image) means liking yourself. Something that sounds so easy is very hard for many people. But liking yourself is one of the most important things you can ever do. If you

47

don't like yourself, how can you expect anyone else to like you? Not only do we all need friends, but we all need to be our own best friend.

Some people seem to be born with high self-esteem, but self-esteem is not inherited. If we could measure self-esteem, we would probably find that John in chapter 1 has higher self-esteem than Brian in our most recent example. For one thing, John's parents are more nurturing and encouraging than Brian's. But don't give up: Even if you don't have much self-esteem now, you can get it. It's hard work, but worth the effort.

You Might Have Tourette Syndrome, But You Are Not Tourette Syndrome

Tic disorders, Tourette syndrome, and associated conditions cause some people to feel bad about themselves. People develop low self-esteem for a variety of reasons: from childhood abuse, parental neglect, or because of a chronic condition such as a tic disorder or ADHD.

The person with high self-esteem might be a person with Tourette syndrome. (Studies have shown that high self-esteem is unrelated to the severity of the tic disorder.) People with high self-esteem understand that there is no one else quite like them; they are unique individuals who don't want to be like anyone else. They want to be themselves. They believe they have a lot to offer the world, and they do.

Maybe because of tics, ADHD, or OCD—or all of the above—you've grown up thinking you can't be happy. You have TS; you're different. Well, you are different. We're all different; that's the fun of being a person.

Remember that even if you do have tics, you are not a tic. You may have Tourette syndrome, but you don't have to let anyone call you a "Touretter"—unless you like that name. It's like calling an adopted person an "adoptee." The term "adoptee" describes only one part of the adopted person much like Tourette syndrome is only one part of a person's life.

How to Learn to Like Yourself

Challenge Irrational Beliefs and Stereotypes

Stereotypes are oversimplified (or just plain wrong) opinions and beliefs. Does it make sense to judge people negatively based on inherited conditions or other aspects of their appearance over which they have no control? And yet, we stereotype all the time. Sometimes we make irrational judgments about people based on their skin color or on the amount of money they have. Some people stereotype those who use crutches or wheelchairs.

The first step in raising your self-esteem is to resolve not to make these judgments about anyone, including yourself. Understand that there is nothing you cannot do because of TS.

Several years ago, the Tourette Syndrome Association told the story of Jeff Bethiany, age twenty-eight, of Fort Thomas, Kentucky. Bethiany, a person with TS, was at the time in training for the Olympics. He shared some of his thoughts on self-esteem: "My philosophy may sound simplistic, but it works. You've got to believe in yourself and your ability to function." For those who believe their particular case of Tourette syndrome is worse than anyone else's, he adds, "You've got to let yourself and the whole world know that you're trying your best and then believe that you can accomplish what you've set out to do."

Accept and Acknowledge Your Emotions

When a doctor says you have Tourette syndrome, you may freak out. People report feeling confusion, fear, anger, denial, or shame. When Dr. Garrett said that Brian did not have Tourette syndrome, Brian felt a great sense of relief. Other people might feel relieved when a doctor says they do have Tourette syndrome because finally someone has given a name to their symptoms. Brian's mother felt anger because she had expected a diagnosis of TS and a pill to "cure" whatever she thought was wrong with her son.

Feel your emotions, then acknowledge and accept them. Give them a name if you can and say something aloud. It's healthy to speak to the mirror. Say "I feel angry" or "I'm scared." Feelings are neither good nor bad; they're normal.

Grieving is part of the process of accepting your diagnosis. Some young people grieve a loss of independence—perhaps a life free of medications. Others must accept the fact that in one respect at least, they are different from their friends. But after allowing yourself a chance to grieve, it's time to move on.

Develop a Skill

One way of moving on is to develop a skill. Over the years certain sports personalities have become TS legends. Baseball player Jim Eisenreich and basketball player Mahmoud Abdul-Rauf both have Tourette syndrome. Both also seem to have inherited athletic abilities that enabled them to excel in professional sports. In 1992, Alan Levitt interviewed Abdul-Rauf for the Tourette Syndrome Association's newsletter. The basketball player said, "God gives you an infirmity, but He also gives you a strength. For me, my weakness may be Tourette, but for my strength, He's given me basketball and the knowledge to understand people—and the ability to understand myself. Whether you are a basketball player or an artist, it's up to you to find that strength and deal with it to overcome your weakness."

But even with inherited abilities, great athletes don't succeed without determination and hard work. Jeff Bethiany worked nights during his Olympic training. He filled his days with a rigorous fitness schedule.

You don't have to become a professional athlete; few people do. But you can get pretty good at almost any sport. Young people with Tourette syndrome often excel at wrestling, gymnastics, or karate, for example. If you like team sports, don't forget basketball, softball, football, soccer, rugby, volleyball, and lacrosse, to name a few. If you prefer individual sports, you might want to try swimming, tennis, weight lifting, fencing, in-line skating, roller-skating, ice-skating, rock climbing, bowling, golfing, snowboarding or skiing, biking, jogging, dancing, or aerobics. If you consider yourself to be a minor (or major) klutz or are afraid to jump into an activity in which you consider yourself at a disadvantage, try talking your parents into a few private or group lessons.

Parents often make sure their young children get into some kind of sport. But as people get older, they may forget that exercise is good, not only for their bodies and their moods, but also for their self-esteem.

If your tics are severe and take you "out of the running" for athletics, remember that sports aren't the only activities you can enjoy and become good at. The list is almost endless.

Felicia was a little actress from the day of her birth. Although she had a tic disorder and ADHD, she took gymnastics and auditioned for plays through middle school and on into high school. Sometimes she got a good part, and sometimes she didn't. She never forgot the words of her high school drama teacher: "There are no small parts, only small actors." Felicia even wrote plays and staged dramatic productions for underprivileged children. In college, she majored in drama and had a minor in stagecraft. Now at age twenty-four, Felicia is an assistant stage manager for a traveling Broadway musical.

Stephen DiJoseph is a pianist and jazz composer who happens to have Tourette syndrome. In the spring 2001 newsletter of the Tourette Syndrome Association, he gives this advice: "I would say to the kids with TS who want to achieve something artistically, to reach for quality in what you're doing—TS or not."

Newspapers and newsletters have featured young people with Tourette syndrome for their abilities in spelling, creative writing, playing musical instruments, singing, acting, and participation in all kinds of athletics. The list goes on and on.

Although becoming proficient at something might increase your self-esteem, you don't have to excel. Just try something new once in a while and see how good the risk-taking makes you feel. What new things could you try? Skydiving? Tightrope walking? Belly dancing? It really doesn't matter; try whatever appeals to you.

Carrie had just graduated from high school. Because she wasn't ready to go back to school, she'd decided to earn some money. Without any particular skills, she ended up working in a video store. As a skinny girl with tics, ADHD, and OCD, she was self-conscious and hated going out with other people, especially those she didn't know.

Most of her friends were away at college, and Carrie felt lost and without direction. To make matters worse, one of her coworkers told her she needed to "get some muscles." In one of her good moods, Carrie agreed to go with this coworker to an open house on lifting weights at a local recreation center.

The night of the open house, Carrie did not want to go. She couldn't decide what to wear. She knew that whatever she did wear would reveal her skinny arms and legs. How much more comfortable it would be to stay home and watch TV. But at the last minute, Carrie threw on a sweat suit and gave herself a push out the door.

Guess what? She had fun. No one looked at her body or her tics. The other people there were just as new and just as worried about how they came across. Her abdominal muscles and leg muscles ached the next day, but Carrie knew she'd done something good for herself. She promised her friend she'd go back on Tuesday and Thursday nights as well as on Saturday mornings.

If you're trying to make some changes, the following guidelines will help.

↪ Believe in yourself. You can do it; you can change.

↪ Be specific. Write down the changes you want to make. Post them on the refrigerator door or on your bulletin board.

↪ Talk positively to yourself. Say aloud, "I can do it. I can change my beliefs about myself. I may not be in charge of my tics, but I am in charge of my life."

↪ Think about and visualize how you will feel after you make your positive changes.

↪ If you fall back, don't beat yourself up. Don't quit. Keep trying. Pick yourself up and start again. You've already made progress, and you can make more.

↪ Even if you don't change anything, love yourself. If you like yourself, others will like you, too. In the end, self-esteem comes from inside, not from someone or something outside. Self-love is good.

A little self-esteem goes a long way, and more is better—for anyone. But for those with Tourette syndrome and associated conditions, getting self-esteem might take hard work.

Coping with Depression

OK, self-esteem works wonders. But what if you don't have it, and you can't seem to get it? What if you're down-right depressed? Realize that depression is not unusual for someone coping with the challenges of Tourette syndrome and associated conditions. Ups and downs—sometimes called mood swings—affect everyone at one time or another. Sometimes bad moods come on for no apparent reason. At other times, you can find a good reason. Maybe you flunked a test. Maybe someone made a mean remark that you overheard. Something like "Look at that psycho. What's wrong with him?" Or maybe you had a fight with a good friend.

Usually people bounce back from these kinds of bad feelings. They feel out of sorts and get quiet or crabby for a day or so and then get over it. But if your low-down feelings hold you back or last for a long time, you might be suffering from clinical depression. The addition of the word "clinical" to the word "depression" implies you might need to do something about your depression, such as going to a clinic or seeing a doctor. A severe depression is sometimes called major depressive disorder (MDD).

Kinds of Depression

Mental health professionals categorize types of depression in different ways. The American Psychiatric Association's *Diagnostic and Statistical Manual of Mental Disorders, 4th Edition*, sometimes called the DSM-IV, gives details. The main thing to remember is that depression occurs on a continuum from ordinary "down moods" to severe, crippling mental illness. Some of the facts doctors look at are (1) how long you've felt depressed, (2) how much your depression affects your life, and (3) how "down" you really feel. For this section, we'll consider most kinds of depression together and put bipolar disorder (sometimes called manic-depressive illness) in a separate category.

Signs of Depression

Depression shows up in different ways. When you think of depression, do you see a mental picture of a person unable to get out of bed in the morning, someone who slogs around with slumped shoulders, a person who locks himself or herself in the bedroom? All of that is possible. But acting sad is not the only way young people show depression. Some start arguments or get themselves in lots of trouble. (Of course, aggressive tendencies can appear with TS or ADHD and do not always indicate depression.) Some people show their depression by smoking or by using alcohol or illegal drugs. Some sleep all the time; others can't sleep. Some people eat too much; others eat too little.

With bipolar disorder, a person's mood goes from pole to pole—from high (manic) to low (depressed). In the euphoric period (or manic phase), people might need little sleep; have exaggerated ideas about their own importance and abilities; be irritable and distractible; engage in impulsive behaviors, such as gambling, promiscuous sex, binge drinking, or the use of illegal drugs; and exhibit other inappropriate behaviors. If this sounds like fun, it isn't. If a person isn't treated during the manic phase, he or she might plunge into a severe depression.

How About You?

Possible causes of depression are biochemical imbalances in the brain combined with a person's psychological and genetic makeup. Factor in individual responses to life's problems, and you have a complicated situation that might be clinical depression.

As with TS, ADHD, OCD, and many other conditions, there are no commonly used laboratory tests to diagnose depression. Because the diagnosis is not always simple, one of the best ways to figure out possible triggers for your depression is to ask yourself, "What's going on in my life?" If, for example, your dad died three months ago, you have a good reason to feel sad. You are grieving the loss of your father. Grief is the normal pain of a great loss. But if the pain never lessens, you may have "complicated grief," which can lead to depression. Losses, even small ones, such as the loss of a wallet or a stolen bike, can cause depression. Other possible triggers of depression include the following.

⮑ Having to move to a new city and/or school

⮑ Breaking up with a girlfriend or boyfriend

⮑ Feeling that you can't "measure up" and never will

⮑ Being unable to communicate with parents or frequently arguing with them

➪ Experiencing parents' arguments, separation, or divorce

➪ Having failures or difficulties in school

Add to these factors a chronic condition such as TS—something that makes you feel "different" or that forces you to put up with teasing or rude comments—and you'll need support. You might find yourself asking questions like these: How will I make it in the job world? How will I do in college? Will I even get into college? As a matter of fact, how am I going to get through high school? Will I ever succeed?

Mental health professionals have known for a long time that a sense of helplessness or lack of power over one's body or life can contribute to depression. Because much of Tourette syndrome is out of your control, you might become depressed at times. But depression doesn't need to rule your life any more than Tourette syndrome needs to rule your life. In a game of cards, you'll get some bad hands, but what you do about those hands is the important part. Although TS may be your "bad hand," how you react will make the difference.

In the preface to their book, *Tourette Syndrome—Tics, Obsessions, Compulsions,* authors James Leckman and Donald Cohen compare Tourette syndrome to a war. They call this war a siege, a "siege against the self." The siege comes in the form of unwanted urges, images, and thoughts. Leckman and Cohen have observed that people with Tourette syndrome often feel as if there is a battle going on inside their heads. The urge inside a person's head tells him to "tic" when he wants to stay still. He wants to win the battle, but he often feels he is losing. Yet, some people are able to move on with their lives, and those who do feel like winners.

Why is it that some people with huge life problems don't become depressed, while others become depressed for no apparent reason? Who knows? Your depression is unique, just as you are unique. Everyone is different.

Another reason for depression is heredity; sometimes depression runs in families. The tendency toward depression might be in your genetic makeup just like TS, ADHD, or OCD. For example, if your mom and her mom suffered from depression along with two of your uncles, you might have inherited a tendency toward depression.

Strategies for Dealing with Depression

People with severe depression don't feel like doing much of anything, including activities they used to enjoy. Maybe they feel tired all the time and are unable to concentrate or make decisions.

A person with heavy-duty depression might think of death and dying all the time—even of suicide. Suicide is the third highest cause of death for those in the fifteen- to twenty-four-year-old age range. Experts estimate that at one time or another at least 60 percent of high school students have thought about suicide.

If you ever feel suicidal (begin to think specific thoughts about ending your life), get help! Call 911, a crisis hotline, your doctor, or the emergency room of a hospital. Don't keep the thoughts to yourself. Tell someone who will take them seriously.

Aaron, age sixteen, who has TS and ADHD, says he would never kill himself. But he has felt low enough to wish he hadn't been born. He says it's somehow comforting to think that other young people have had similar feelings. People who consider suicide believe they've run out of choices in their lives. In truth, they haven't; there are always options.

Whenever Jessica feels rotten about herself or has a problem that defies solution, she remembers her minister saying, "You always have options; you may not think so, but you do." Everyone has someone who cares. You may not think so, but there is someone out there for you. Saying to yourself, "My family would be better off without me," is untrue. Even if a statement seems true at the time, the situation is bound to change with time.

No matter what kind of depression you have and however it shows itself, acknowledging it is an important first step in getting rid of it. Imagine yourself tipping your hat to your depression and saying, "Hi. How can I get rid of you?"

If people start showing concern about you, don't just blow them off. It's OK and even healthy to say, "I'm feeling kind of down today," or "I'm in a crabby mood," or "I've been feeling sad for a long time, and I'm getting sick of it," or "I need help!" If you don't admit to feelings of depression or sadness, you can't help yourself, and no one else can help you either. Remember that feelings are important; without them we wouldn't be human.

How can you shake depression? First, there is our old friend exercise. There are also supports like friends or church. Get plenty of rest and try not to become overloaded with too many school activities. Here are a few more coping strategies.

Aim for Flexibility

Many depressed people feel trapped inside themselves. They aren't flexible enough to see their options. Chances are you're aware of your own inflexibility. What can you do about it? One thing you can do is to drop words such as "should," "ought," and "have to" from your vocabulary. These are words of inflexibility. When you don't measure up to your own rigid standards, you feel terrible.

Rob never thought he was measuring up. As a result, he felt depressed. His thoughts included, "I should work out every day" (he didn't, which made him feel bad), "I have to get a 4.0 average or I'll never get into college" (when he got a B in calculus, he felt terrible), and "I ought to have a girlfriend by now."

Try to have flexible thoughts and beliefs about yourself. Use phrases such as "I'll try to," "I hope I can," or "I want to, if possible."

Take Care of Yourself

Don't say, "I should take care of myself." Rather, give yourself permission to do so. It's OK to be a bit selfish now and then. And while you're at it, learn to say no, when necessary.

> People at school knew they could go to Sadie for help. Need help decorating the cafeteria? Ask Sadie. Need someone to work in the carnival's teacher-dunking booth? Ask Sadie. Need someone to deliver Thanksgiving baskets to the needy? Ask Sadie. Partly as a result of doing everything for everyone except herself, Sadie had tics that were out of control; she felt as if she were coming unglued. Sadie needed to learn to say no.
>
> She could say, "I think I'd like to go running today instead of decorating" or "I've decided to stay home and watch a movie tonight."

Look for a Bright Side

There are two ways of looking at most daily happenings— the bright (positive) side and the dark (negative) side. To help keep depression at bay, cultivate bright-side thinking.

> On a sunny afternoon, Alexandra took a "maiden voyage" with her parents' car. She had gotten her license the day before. When she offered to go to the store to get some lettuce for her parents' dinner party that night, she could almost hear them thinking, "It's only a couple of miles. How much damage can she do?"

She backed carefully out of the narrow driveway and took the main drag to the store. As she passed her favorite bagel place, she glanced over to see if it was open. Thud! In that instant, she had crashed her parents' car into the car ahead of her, which had braked for a cat crossing the road.

Shaking, Alexandra got out to survey the damage. "Oh, I'm so sorry," she said. "Are you OK?"

"I'm OK and you're OK," said the lady. "That's the main thing, isn't it?" They exchanged information. Alexandra's car had no damage, but the lady's back bumper was dented and scratched. Before they parted, the lady gave Alexandra a hug.

But Alexandra's day was ruined. "Our insurance rates will go way up," she thought. "Mom and Dad will never let me use the car again. If only I hadn't looked over. If only I'd taken a different street. If only that cat hadn't crossed the road. If only I hadn't gone at all."

By the next day, though, after telling a few people about her accident, Alexandra was able to look on the bright side: (1) No one was hurt; (2) the damage was minor; (3) the lady was understanding; (4) they'd both worn their seat belts; (5) her parents hadn't been too mad and didn't give her a lecture; and (6) she'd survived and learned some important lessons.

Be Grateful and Quick to Forgive

If you're a person who says prayers, pray with thankfulness in mind. In other words, put the emphasis on what you have rather than on what you don't have. It's amazing how much better this simple act of thankfulness will make you feel. If you don't pray, you can still be thankful. Make it a habit to stop several times a day, look around you, and give thanks for the good things you enjoy. If you're running, give thanks for your legs. If you're swimming, be grateful for the water surrounding you and the opportunity to act like a fish. If you're eating, be thankful for crunchy fries or a gooey banana split.

And while you're in a thankful frame of mind, try to forgive those who have hurt you. Include forgiveness for yourself. Nobody's perfect. Forgiving is much more healthy and uplifting than nursing a grudge.

Get Help

The previous suggestions will help anyone, especially those who fight depression. However, if you have real, honest-to-goodness clinical depression, you may need help from a trained, objective person (someone outside your family). Clinical depression is not usually something you can snap out of. Even if depression does eventually go away, it may come back—unless you get help. Untreated depressions of all kinds tend to re-cycle. When they come back, they may be worse than they were before. The sooner you get treatment, the sooner you'll get better.

Various types of counseling, which we'll discuss in the next chapter, are used to treat depression. Recent years have seen an explosion in different kinds of medications used to treat depression. The right kind of medication prescribed by a knowledgeable physician can make a big difference, especially if used in combination with the right kind of psychotherapy.

Antidepressant medications appear to help correct the neurochemical imbalances in the brain that lead to depression. Mentioned earlier, selective serotonin reuptake inhibitors include Prozac, Zoloft, Paxil, and Luvox. Older medications used for depression are the tricyclic antidepressants. Examples are Tofranil, Norpramin, Pamelor, and Elavil. Doctors usually treat manic depression with Eskalith (lithium), Depakote (valproic acid), or Tegretol (carbamazepine).

Now that we've talked about the challenges of living with tics and Tourette syndrome, let's talk about some positive actions a person with Tourette syndrome can take to help get through life happily. One of the main things is support. In the next chapter, we'll go over some of the supports available.

Support: Get It— Wherever and Whenever You Can Find It

Few of us would want to live alone in a cave. Most of us need other people to help us through life. If you have a chronic condition, such as Tourette syndrome, support is even more important. Where can you get support and what kind is out there?

Informal Supports

Family

Introduce stress—such as the stress of TS—into any family system, and the whole family needs to make adjustments. A family therapist, Virginia Satir, compares families to mobiles. When stress causes movement or change to one part of the mobile (or family), the other parts must move and change, too.

Tourette syndrome pushes its way into a family with abrupt movements and sounds. There's no way other family members or the person with TS can ignore motor and verbal tics. A family with open communication is likely to do whatever is necessary to stay mentally healthy. A family with negative or no communication among members might start to pull apart or fall apart.

If the person with TS notices what is happening and feels guilty, the family will suffer even more. If you're the person with Tourette syndrome, you may find it hard to keep in mind that TS is not your fault. It's not the fault of your mother or father; it's not the fault of your brother or sister. In some families, brothers or sisters might feel guilty because one child has TS and they don't.

During times of stress in a family (for example, after a diagnosis of TS, when tics get worse for a time, or when school or behavior problems cause disagreements), family therapy can help. (We'll talk more about family therapy later.)

Remember that resentments are common in all families. At one time or another, almost all brothers and sisters have felt that someone else gets more attention. Your siblings may feel that you (the child with TS) are getting more than your share of your parents' attention. Or, because TS, ADHD, and OCD tend to run in families, you might feel envious that one of your siblings is getting more attention than you are. You may feel resentment toward a sibling you consider "normal." Sometimes when a parent takes a child to the doctor because of tics, the parent discovers that he or she has tics, Tourette syndrome, or ADHD and didn't know it. That parent may then feel resentful about his or her own condition in addition to feeling guilt or resentment about yours. Tourette syndrome can use up a lot of everyone's time and energy, and everyone in the family may feel there is simply not enough energy to go around. Some families are able to talk about these feelings; others are not. Again, many families will find a few sessions of family counseling or a support group for "hurting members" to be a great help.

In a parent support group, Darla confided that if her son with TS has had a bad day at school, he wants to quit. He has a hard time problem solving or even admitting that everyone has bad days. For Darla, it was comforting to see other heads nodding as she told her son's story.

At the beginning of the school year, Andy told his story in a teen support group. In his big, new high school, he'd found it impossible to get from one class to another without going back to the original home-room. As a result, he was always late for the next class. But even worse than the original problem was having his mom come to school one day to lead him through the maze.

Friends

In addition to having friends within our families, we need friends outside the family. In the book *Don't Think About Monkeys,* John Hilkevich, one of the book's editors, intro-duces the idea of making friends with your own Tourette syndrome. He calls Tourette syndrome "both a curse and a gift" and says TS has not only isolated him but also con-nected him to others.

Coeditor Adam Ward Seligman discusses the Tourette "brotherhood" or "community." Anyone who has ever attended a TS support group will be able to understand this concept.

Finally, in the same collection of stories, a young man, Mitchell Vitiello, talks about making friends and how he went about it. One year at camp, when he was feeling particularly down and his Tourette syndrome was flaring up, he called home. The advice his father gave him was to act as if his tics didn't bother him. If the problem didn't bother Mitchell, his father said, it wouldn't bother anyone else. Mitchell took his father's advice. This advice, which he used from then on, changed his life.

Psychotherapy

Chances are that unless you're out of high school, you're not going to be choosing a therapist or a type of therapy— your parents are. And chances are that you don't want to go—you don't like "shrinks," you're too busy, or you're not "crazy." Of course you're not. But sometimes family and friends are too close. They talk too much and don't listen enough. Their suggestions might annoy you; you may have heard everything they have to say a hundred times. Maybe you need a good listener or some objective advice. A few sessions with a counselor or a series of group meetings can help. How does anyone get through the maze and know what kind of counselor to get? It may help if you understand some of the principles underlying the different kinds of therapy.

What you might not know is that therapy is about communication—and how to get better at it. A therapist or a group can give you (along with support) tools for valuing yourself and for getting along better with others (who, in turn, will give you support).

Types of Therapists
People with different amounts of training and different philosophies work as therapists.

➩ Psychiatrists are medical doctors with four years of college plus four years of medical school along with four more years of psychiatric residency. These doctors (with M.D. after their names) are the only therapists who can prescribe medications.

↪ Licensed clinical psychologists usually have four years of college plus at least four years of graduate school. In their training, which includes an internship, they learn how to do psychological assessments and testing, as well as counseling. They will have initials such as Ph.D. or Psy.D. after their names.

↪ Licensed clinical social workers (L.C.S.W.s) have earned a master's degree in social work, plus one or two years of additional supervised training before they take their licensing exam.

↪ Family therapists usually have degrees as psychiatrists, psychologists, or social workers with additional training in helping people solve problems within their families. Other people with special training in counseling include ministers, licensed professional counselors (L.P.C.s), and psychiatric nurses.

↪ Life coaches like to help people get their lives on track by looking "outside the box" with supportive suggestions and goal-setting activities. Life coaches come from various disciplines. Currently this profession is not strictly regulated, so be certain to check the person's qualifications and experience.

Therapists not only have different professional backgrounds but also different personalities and ways of working with people. Some directly offer helpful insights and suggestions; others are nondirective, helping you arrive at your own conclusions. Neither of these approaches is better than the other; it just depends on what works best for you. After one or two visits, you should be able to tell whether you feel comfortable with a certain therapist. If not, you can get other recommendations and try someone else.

Your therapist should give you a disclosure form that includes a record of his or her philosophy, training, and methods of working. You or your parents have probably gotten a list of therapists from a reputable organization, such as your local Tourette Syndrome Association. Make sure you are working with a person who has knowledge of Tourette syndrome and experience with co-occurring conditions.

Counseling Types

Individual Therapy

Individual therapy is just you and the counselor, a one-on-one relationship. This situation will be helpful for you if you don't feel comfortable in a group setting. The counselor will make an agreement with you to keep what you say confidential.

Try calling your local chapter of the Tourette Syndrome Association and see whether you can receive some names of therapists familiar with TS. If you're taking medication, a medical doctor (psychiatrist, neurologist, pediatrician, adolescent medicine specialist, or family doctor) will have to monitor your medications. Working one-on-one with a counselor can be a great way to start talking about feelings and getting ideas for changing behaviors.

Family Therapy

Family therapy brings the most important people from your immediate world together to solve problems.

Usually it's very hard to get a group of busy people together for an hour each week, but you'll probably find it is worth the trouble.

Everyone in the family gets involved, not just the identified patient. Not everyone has to go every time. Sometimes the therapist might want to see everyone, sometimes the therapist meets with all the kids, or just the parents, or just the parents and the child with TS. Sometimes the therapist might want to include grandparents, cousins, or aunts and uncles.

The family, together with the family therapist, will identify goals for the family and the people in it. Examples of possible goals are healthy communication among all family members, more appreciation of each other, increased self-esteem for everyone, taking pressure off the person with TS, more attention for those who don't have TS, the opening up and acknowledgment of family secrets, how to have more fun with the family, and any number of other mutually agreed upon goals.

Support Groups

Support groups come in all sizes and types. Some groups have a professional leader; other groups have a volunteer leader. Some groups rotate leadership among members. There are support groups for people with TS, support groups for brothers and sisters of people with TS, and support groups for parents of people with TS. One mother at a recent support group said her thirteen-year-old son is very open about his Tourette syndrome. She recently heard him say to a friend, "Do you want to come with us to my tic group?"

One main benefit of a support group is finding out you are not alone. In a support group, you'll make friends with people who have similar issues and concerns. Another benefit is picking up pieces of wisdom and coping techniques.

Bernie, who was against taking medications for his tics, recently attended his first support group. Most of the other kids there had tried medication at one time or another and found medications took the edge off their tics. A lot of people laughed and said they didn't know if their tics had gone away because of the meds or if they had just decided to go away on their own. Some of the following topics are likely to come up.

➭ How to deal with curious, nosy, or rude people

➭ How to deal with the school system or various parts of it

➭ How it feels to get teased or laughed at and what to do about it

➭ How it feels to be excluded from an activity for whatever reason

➭ How to find someone who cares who is not your parent

➭ How to get a job

Where can you go to find a support group? The first step is to join the national Tourette Syndrome Association and/or your local chapter. Paying dues to the national organization automatically makes you a member of your state or local group. Tourette syndrome is less common than ADHD. If you can't find a TS support group near you, you might want to try an ADHD support group. Many of the problems are similar. Some of the organizations listed in the back of this book will help you to find local resources.

You can also try your local children's hospital, your physician, a teacher, or a social worker. Any of these people might be able to lead you to resources. Another possible resource is a TS camp. This type of camp is likely to be available in your area for only one week every year, and it may be for young kids. But you might be able to do volunteer work there, giving support as well as getting it.

If you live in a small community or find yourself isolated from other people with Tourette syndrome, try the Internet. Many chapters of the Tourette Syndrome Association have their own Web pages. You might also be able to find support and give-and-take on a cyber forum, newsgroup, or chat room even though you're not physically in the same room with your supporters.

Stress-Reduction Techniques

Stress reduction will not cure Tourette syndrome, but reducing your stress level can help. People often choose (or fall into) negative habits to reduce stress. Smoking, drinking, using illegal drugs, and engaging in unprotected, promiscuous sexual activities are all unhealthy ways of relieving stress. These addictive behaviors cause more problems than they solve and add to a person's stress level. Many experts believe people with Tourette syndrome are more susceptible to addictions than other people. So beware. Don't start.

One of the best and most healthy ways to relieve stress is to exercise, which we discussed earlier, under self-esteem boosters. Exercise not only relieves stress and increases self-esteem, but it also relieves depression and is good for your body.

Other healthy de-stressors include—but are not limited to—affirmations, hobbies, journaling, massage/touch, meditation, relaxation techniques, visualization/imagery, and volunteer work. Pick one of these de-stressors and see whether it works for you. If it doesn't, drop it and try another one. You can use several of the de-stressors at any time. Your family members might enjoy trying them, too.

Affirmations

Formulating, saying, and believing affirmations is good practice for anyone, not only people with Tourette syndrome. Affirmations are positive, present-oriented statements we make to ourselves about ourselves. It's far too easy to become bogged down with negatives: "I'm so clumsy," "I'm too impulsive," "I can't seem to get along with people."

Why not change your focus? Try these positive statements and make up some more of your own.

⮑ I have Tourette syndrome, and I am a healthy person.

⮑ I am a valuable person.

⮑ I give support to others in need.

⮑ I have a great sense of humor.

⮑ I move easily through life.

75

You must be able to believe your affirmations. Otherwise, you'll revert to negative thinking and defeat yourself before you get started. Repeat your affirmations several times each day. Say them in your head, say them aloud, or write them down. But most of all, believe them!

For example, Duane wrote, "I move comfortably through life." Immediately thereafter he said to himself, "No, you don't. You tic and jerk your way through life." With the help of his therapist, Duane changed his affirmation to "I am a good athlete," which he was.

Hobbies

Tics decrease in most people when they are engaged in something that is interesting to them as well as fun. A hobby doesn't have to be something you're the best at. A hobby can be anything you enjoy doing.

Those with compulsive tendencies make great collectors. It doesn't matter what you collect—baseball cards, stamps, rocks, or matchbooks—as long as you enjoy the process. Dr. Carl Bennett, the surgeon featured in Oliver Sacks's book *An Anthropologist on Mars,* collects sounds. Sacks reports that Bennett's sons help their father to collect unusual names, which Bennett keeps in lists. He calls these words and sounds "candy for the mind."

Journaling

For some people keeping a journal (or daily log) is a great diversion, an activity that rounds out each day. For others, even the idea of writing in a daily journal raises

Socialization Groups

Socialization groups, or "social skills" groups, can also be supportive. These groups, which are more common in big cities, give people with TS a chance to practice interactions with others. Are you a person who makes friends easily but then loses them just as easily? Have you noticed you have a way of turning people off? Do you feel bad about yourself and believe you don't deserve to have friends? Do you find yourself wanting to stay home from school and/or social occasions because you don't know how to act?

If you answered yes to any of these questions, you would benefit from a socialization group. Socialization groups often use role-playing as a way of reinforcing social skills. Here's an example of an exchange that took place in Zach's recent group.

> *Melissa is telling group members about not getting a part in the school play, but she has gone on and on for several minutes, and the group is getting restless.*
> *Zach: Shut up, Melissa. You talk too long.*
> *Melissa sticks out her tongue.*
> *Melissa: Zach, you brat! Who asked you?*
> *Zach leans over and yanks Melissa's ponytail.*
> *Melissa screams and stomps on Zach's toe.*
> *Mr. Ross, a licensed clinical social worker: Wait a minute. Let's go over that again. Zach, could you visualize a more effective way of telling Melissa she had used up her talking time?*
> *Zach: Well, I guess I could have said, "Be quiet," instead of "Shut up."*

Mr. Ross: Anything else?

Zach: I suppose I could have said, "Please, be quiet."

Mr. Ross: Anything else?

Zach: I don't know. Maybe I should have used an "I" message.

Mr. Ross: How about an example?

Zach: I could have said, "I get tired when I have to listen for a long time."

Mr. Ross: Excellent work, Zach. How about you, Melissa?

Melissa: I interrupted. But he hurt my feelings.

Mr. Ross: Can you think of another way you could have responded?

Melissa: I guess I should have said something like, "Please let me finish."

Mr. Ross: Good! Now let's try that exchange again.

their stress and dread levels. But unlike completing a test, there are no right or wrong answers to write in your journal. Here are some suggestions.

- ↪ Keep a tic journal. Record what you think might have triggered your tics. Such a record can be useful in deciding which, if any, situations to avoid. It might also be helpful when you meet with a doctor or other health professional.

⮑ Write down what happened in your day. Be sure to focus on the good as well as the bad. Even more important, how did you feel about what happened? What made you happy? What made you sad?

⮑ If you want to, keep a record of your dreams and try to figure out what they mean.

⮑ Do some goal setting. Write down short-term goals. Kevin's first short-term goal was to invite Angel to the junior prom three weeks down the road. (He did, and she accepted.) An intermediate goal was to give his TS medication a three-month trial. A long-term goal was to fill out several college applications.

Massage

Massage is one type of therapeutic touch. Some people pay big bucks to get a massage. But you don't have to. If a friend or family member asks what you want for your birthday, say, "a massage, please." You don't need a professional to rub your sore muscles. Tell your "massage therapist" what feels good, where to apply more pressure or less.

Cal's mother kept a tic journal that she shared with the doctor. "Turns his head to the left, almost to the point of looking behind him. Repeats this movement several times a day. Especially noticeable when skiing, both cross-country and downhill. Somewhat dangerous when going downhill. Started piano lessons after Christmas. Same movement is frequent. Says his neck is always sore. Enjoys the neck and back massages I give when I can."

Something that works for some people, especially those with TS plus ADHD, is to do the "sandwich maneuver."

Wrap yourself in a blanket and get someone else to put pressure on you in the form of pillows. A bit later, have that person give you a back massage.

If you decide you'd like a professional massage, get recommendations from friends, recreation leaders, or health clubs. There are many different types of massage. Find out if the massage therapist you're considering is certified and/or if he or she received training at a nationally accredited school of massage therapy. Does he or she belong to a national organization such as the American Massage Therapy Association or the American Oriental Bodywork Therapy Association?

Meditation

The goal of meditation is to produce relaxation, inner peace, and increased awareness. Meditation can take many forms. To begin the process of meditation, you might sit on a straight chair with your feet touching the floor. Some people sit cross-legged on the floor. Others lie on their backs. After figuring out which body posture you want to use, decide what you will do during your meditation time. Some people concentrate on their breathing—inhaling, exhaling. They allow no intrusive thoughts. Other people say a mantra, which is a repeated sound said (inwardly or outwardly) over and over. Some people say a prayer.

Quieting the racing of the mind by focusing on one thing (the breath, a mantra, or a prayer) for about twenty minutes each day brings peace to many people.

"Mindfulness," in which you keep your mind entirely focused on the present, is another form of meditation. For example, while peeling potatoes, think only of peeling potatoes—not what you're wearing to school the next day. Listen to the scraping sound of the peeler, watch the potato change from brown to white as the skin is peeled away, feel the firmness of the vegetable you're holding.

Movement is a part of some forms of meditation. Examples are tai chi and yoga. Tai chi is a form of Chinese movement therapy. It is considered one of the "soft" martial arts because it is based on relaxation, yielding, and nonaggression. Yoga is an ancient Indian system of muscle exercises, postures, and breathing techniques. It stretches, strengthens, and relaxes. The word "yoga" means "union." Its goal is self-control, focusing the mind, quieting the emotions, and renewing the body.

Some people also meditate and calm themselves by doing other forms of martial arts, as well as walking, dancing, or listening to music.

Relaxation

The subject of relaxation covers a lot of territory. What is relaxing for one person might be hard work for another. The basis for almost all relaxation techniques is abdominal or diaphragmatic breathing. Everyone breathes, right? The trouble is that most of us don't breathe in a way that eliminates tension. We take tiny, shallow breaths that begin and end in our chests. What we need to learn is deep breathing that starts and ends in the abdomen.

While you're lying on your back (or sitting in a chair or on the floor with your legs crossed), put one hand on your abdomen and the other on your chest. Now inhale slowly and deeply through your nose. Breathing this way should make your abdomen (and your hand) rise. After a few seconds, exhale through your mouth. As you breathe out, your abdomen should sink. Try to relax your muscles and concentrate on your breathing. The hand on your chest shouldn't move. This kind of breathing gets carbon dioxide out of your blood, causing you to feel more alert and less stressed.

Another type of relaxation exercise that can help people with Tourette syndrome is called progressive muscle relaxation. It is easy to do. Lie on your back on a bed or on the floor. (Don't get too comfortable and fall asleep!) The idea is to tense individual muscles for a certain time and then relax them. Figure out a time period that seems to work for each muscle tensing. How about seven seconds? Start with your head and face. Scrunch up your face muscles and hold this grimace for seven seconds. Now relax. Pucker up your lips (like you're kissing someone). Relax. Move down to your shoulders. Squeeze them up to your ears and hold them there for seven seconds. Relax. Now pull your arms tightly to your sides for seven seconds. Let go. Clench your fists for seven seconds. Let go. Get the idea? Keep moving down your body, ending with your toes.

Visualization/Imagery

Visualization is the use of imagination to create positive images in our minds. Without even realizing it, most of us make these mental pictures all the time. Haven't you imagined a teacher handing back a paper with a huge A on top? Have you visualized a banana split even before you've ordered it? You can employ the same technique to give yourself a sense of calm and healing.

Get relaxed and comfortable. Close your eyes and imagine a place that is calm and serene. If you like warmth and water, imagine yourself lying on a sun-drenched beach. If you like to watch fish swim, imagine yourself snorkeling in the Caribbean. If you like snow and mountains, imagine yourself gliding effortlessly down a powder-covered slope. Now imagine yourself free of tics. Hold that image.

You can use this technique before getting up in front of the class to give a report or a speech. You can use it before an athletic event you're in or before a job interview. Your only limit is your imagination. Don't give up. You can use guided imagery audiocassettes, which will tell you what to visualize. The music on these tapes will relax almost anyone.

Volunteering

"Hey, I have enough trouble taking care of myself—you're saying I should volunteer to take care of somebody else?"

Yes. It's easy to think you're not able to help others, but that's not true. Helping someone else can pull you out of yourself and make you grateful for life's blessings.

Volunteer to tutor a third-grader in math, go to a nursing home and read to a resident, bake cookies for someone. If you don't want to work directly with people, you could volunteer to mend books at the library or offer your services to Habitat for Humanity to build homes for people with low incomes.

Keep Your Options Open

One or more of these relievers might help you. If not, you might be able to find others with the help of books such as *The Encyclopedia of Healing Therapies*, by Anne Woodham and David Peters, M.D.

Don't expect too much too quickly. Change is hard work and takes time. Do a little something every day. Eventually the small changes in your life will add up to big ones. The main thing to remember is not to fight life's battles alone. Get help.

Strategies for Coping with Tourette Syndrome

Now that you've taken some important steps in addressing the challenges you face, you might be ready to work on even larger action strategies for coping with Tourette syndrome and related conditions.

Here are some suggestions. However, each person must decide for himself or herself what works. Journaling, your therapist, and/or your support group may all be helpful to you in this process of self-discovery.

In the book *Children with Tourette Syndrome*, William Rubin, M.A., suggests trying to develop coping strategies in the following four categories.

- Being out in public

- Dealing with acquaintances

- Relating to "close" people, such as family and good friends

- Accomplishing tasks, such as those at school, in sports, or at a job

Rubin says that projecting an image of competence is important. Your self-esteem will also come in handy in any of these four areas.

When Out and About

Although Rubin doesn't mention the possibility of being stopped by police for one reason or another, it could happen. Therefore, it's best to be prepared with a card that states in bold letters:

I HAVE A MEDICAL CONDITION— TOURETTE SYNDROME

For verification, please call:

➪ Relative's name
➪ Doctor's name

For a dollar, you can get a printed plastic card from the Tourette Syndrome Association. One side provides space for your name and address. The other side gives a simple explanation of the involuntary nature of tic disorders and Tourette syndrome.

Much more likely than the possibility of being stopped by police is the possibility of being teased. Rubin suggests that by ignoring the teaser, you show your competence to others. By acting polite, friendly, and more mature than some people your age, you are revealing yourself as a person to be trusted. You may not feel like being friendly and polite all the time, but at least you can try.

Don't avoid people or public situations unless (1) the situation is likely to make you feel terribly uncomfortable, or (2) your tics will make others very uncomfortable. For example, if you're in a period of severe tics, you might want to avoid fancy restaurants or classical music concerts. In these instances, you might feel so worried about making others uncomfortable that you, in turn, would feel uncomfortable. But having Tourette syndrome, no matter how severe, doesn't mean you have to sit in the basement watching videos every night.

A technique for dealing with other public situations is preparation. Let's use the example of a party. When you're invited to a party, you prepare by taking a shower, picking out nice clothes, putting your clothes on, and doing something with your hair and face to make certain that you're presentable. Imagine that this party is an intergenerational affair at your house and you're expected to help. Go through the whole format of the party with your parents. When will it start? When will it end? What goes on in between? Your job is to take people's coats. Where do you take them? To the hall closet? To a bedroom upstairs? When the party ends, are you expected to retrieve the coats? Find out exactly what you're supposed to do and when. Prepare for movies and restaurants by thinking of the best time to go. If you're with your family, you may all decide to go early during the least crowded times.

Remember Andy (in chapter 5) who had trouble getting from class to class? If Andy or his mother had foreseen this difficulty, he and his mother, or Andy and a school counselor, could have done a practice run from class to class in the days before school started. You can also plan ahead with your daily school schedule or with after-school schedules. Figure out your schedule in thirty-minute time blocks, write it down, and try to stick to it.

Dealing with Acquaintances

In interactions with people you don't know very well, do what makes you feel comfortable. Dave didn't feel comfortable explaining about Tourette syndrome to classmates; on various occasions, he told people he had a twitchy muscle, a cramp in his leg, an itchy mosquito bite, or a sore back. Sometimes, however, it is easier to be up-front and say something like this: "I have Tourette syndrome. It's an inherited condition, but it's not contagious." Or "I have trouble controlling my movements. I can't help it; I have Tourette syndrome." Or "Having tics is like having hiccups. They'll stop eventually." Often Dave didn't feel like saying anything. Let them stare, he thought, and closed his eyes. Some people choose to hand out a printed card that says, "I have Tourette syndrome."

In a college or job interview, you'll probably have an opportunity to explain that you have Tourette syndrome. You might need to do a bit of educating, too, but you don't have to dwell on your condition. It isn't going to affect how well you can do the job. If your potential employer sees you being matter-of-fact about TS, he or she can assume you'll be the same way on the job and with people you meet. In other words, model your competent behavior for your potential employer. If you don't make a big deal of TS, others will assume it's not a big deal. We'll talk more about jobs and interviewing later.

In some encounters with acquaintances, you may decide that the less attention focused on you, the better. However, in other situations, such as living with a college roommate, you may choose to provide some TS education. For a class, you could arrange for a video. (Some are listed in the back of this book.) You could arrange for a simple presentation to your church group. If you have to (or have the opportunity to) participate in a school science fair, you could do a TS project.

If you don't want to put together your own presentation, you can contact your local chapter of the Tourette Syndrome Association to get a skilled volunteer. Experts in such matters suggest that rather than starting with a discussion of TS, the presenter might choose to talk about a well-known medical condition, such as asthma or diabetes. The presenter might ask the students if they know anyone with either of these conditions. What parts of the body do they affect? What's difficult for the person who has these conditions? Many students realize that the person with asthma might need to use an inhaler. A person with diabetes might need to get injections of insulin. Would anyone tease a person who needs to use an inhaler or needs to give himself shots? The presenter can then introduce Tourette syndrome. (The Tourette Syndrome Association, Inc., provides an Educators' In-Service Program on understanding Tourette syndrome that includes a peer-training manual.)

Relating to Close Friends and Relatives

People with Tourette syndrome often walk a fine line. They want to be honest with people close to them. But they also want to avoid making TS the entire focus of their lives—or the lives of people close to them. To a certain extent, all people must perform this balancing act. How does anyone balance what is "me and mine" with what is "you and yours"? How much about any problem do you share with family members and close friends? How much is up to you, but the goal for everyone is honesty.

Gus, age sixteen, had a bad day at school. He'd finally gotten up enough nerve to invite Sara to a school dance. She said she was sorry, but she had to go to her grandmother's. Her grandmother's? Sure. Gus hadn't cried since he was about six years old, but he felt like crying. When he went home after school, he couldn't talk about what had happened. It was his tics, of course. He hated his parents for giving him their genes, he hated his "normal" sister and brother, he hated Sara, he hated life that day. He slammed pots and pans around while making his own dinner and managed to break a glass. His parents, his sister, and his brother tiptoed around him. His mom showed her concern with a hug and a pat on the back, but no one forced Gus to talk. He went to bed early. The next day after school, he felt ready to try to put his thoughts into words. His mom listened without saying much. Gus talked himself into understanding that everyone faces rejection at times. It's a part of living that's no fun. But people survive and so would he. He went back to school the next day and talked to Sara, who became a close friend—if not his date for the dance.

Family members will become frustrated with Tourette syndrome just as you often do. If they blurt out hurtful words, remember that it's TS they're angry with, not you as a person. If one of your motor tics (such as a flinging arm) breaks something or hurts someone, you might hear a parent say a bad word. If verbal tics annoy family members while they're watching TV, try to find a creative solution, such as individual headsets or a second TV.

Accomplishing Tasks

In trying to get things done, one of the most important things is to analyze which symptoms affect what tasks. Before you can figure out what to do about a problem, you must know what is causing the problem. For example, if you're a person whose tics become worse the more tired you are, you might decide to do homework in the early morning rather than late at night. Similarly, if you have a choice in job hours, you might choose an early shift over a late one.

Physical exercise helps on many levels. It can decrease tics in some people, it decreases stress and depression, and it increases self-esteem. Being part of a team in any sport will help you to learn to work with others for a common goal. You get to know your teammates and classmates, and they get to know you.

When you were in elementary school, your parents did most of your educational planning, communicating with the school, and advocating for you. In the teen years, you begin to take more responsibility for your own business. In the "olden days" when you were a kid, your parents figured out strategies to help you to achieve educational goals. But now the job of designing strategies for success is yours. After all, it's your life.

Brittany, age seventeen, wanted to go to college, something no one else in her family had done. One of her friends was using an educational consultant to help with applications and essays. Brittany knew her parents couldn't afford the expense. She also knew that with her TS and associated problems, she would have a hard time doing the application process by herself. She got a summer job and ended up making enough money to pay the consultation fee, which made Brittany and her parents feel good.

Tics can cause problems at school. Obviously if you have an arm or hand tic, writing is difficult. (Find out whether you can use a laptop computer at school. One TS support group rents them to members who need them.) Eye or head tics can interfere with reading. (Books on tape can help at home.) If TS causes a lot of problems at school, you might want to ask your doctor to write a letter to the school district requesting educational accommodations. With the help of a physician's letter, you should be able to access entitlements available under federal, state, or local laws.

If you find that getting up and taking a short break helps with tic-release, try for a seat close to the door. Arrange for a signal to use with your teachers when you need to take a trip to the drinking fountain, rest room, or other special room, such as the social worker's or nurse's office. Also, if your tics seem to get worse as the day goes on, see if you can schedule your most important classes early.

By the time you get to high school and college, you should have some idea about which accommodations work best for the dentist or doctor. If you have TS, you don't need to acquire a mouthful of cavities just because you're embarrassed about moving around a lot in the dental chair. Find doctors and dentists who understand Tourette syndrome. You might be able to get some suggestions from your local TS association.

Now that we've gone over a few strategies to help with tics, let's see what action strategies work for those with attention, impulse, and "hyper" problems.

Strategies for Coping with Tourette Syndrome (Plus Attention Deficit Hyperactivity Disorder)

If up to 60 percent of people with Tourette syndrome also have ADHD, it's important to try to make sense of these complicated disorders when they occur together. (Of course, we're never going to make total sense of them; we'll do better if we just accept some things and get on with life.)

In addition to motor and verbal tics, Caitlyn has ADHD. (Two doctors, Caitlyn's teachers, her parents, and Caitlyn all agree on this.) Not all young people are as articulate or as tuned into their feelings as Caitlyn.

Let's see. Where to start. I guess since I was about five, I've had tics—off and on. But my mom says I've been "hyper" ever since I could move. Compared to ADHD, the tics are only a minor irritation. It's the ADHD that has gotten me into the most trouble over the years. In school, I drive people crazy. If I'm not experiencing tics, my leg is flapping, or I'm talking to the person sitting next to me.

I get easily distracted by almost anything—a bug on the floor, or someone snapping gum, or I'll start thinking about what's for lunch. I've heard that people with ADHD get into a lot of fights. I don't get into fights like slugging people or pulling hair. But somebody will look at me wrong or say something that irritates me. Instead of letting it go, I'll fire off a smart remark. Then I want to bite my tongue. When I was younger, I'd have these temper tantrums that lasted for hours. Well, maybe half an hour. I don't do this anymore. I can't get to sleep at night no matter how hard I try or how late I go to bed. Then I have trouble getting up in the morning. Until I was twelve, I wet the bed almost every night. This drove my mom crazy.

I fall asleep in class. My teachers think I'm acting bored, but I don't mean to. It's the same as when I'm in the car with my mom. She'll be talking away and all of a sudden, she's shaking me to get me to wake up. I just nod off. She thinks I'm tuning her out, which I am, but not on purpose.

Sometimes I think, What the—! I'm never going to be any different. Why try?

In order to understand what happens in ADHD, it can help to consider arousal theory, which can be applied to Caitlyn and some of her difficulties. According to Marilyn Dornbush and Sheryl Pruitt in *Teaching the Tiger*, people with neurological impairments such as TS, ADHD, and OCD rarely have optimal brain arousal. Instead, they are either underaroused (feeling tired; being slow in processing information; being unable to focus or pay attention) or they are overaroused (feeling irritable, angry, aggressive, or frustrated; feeling overstimulated; or feeling confused and unable to finish their work).

No wonder the underaroused person is sluggish in school and doesn't get much work done. On the other hand, overaroused people can overreact and have a hard time functioning in crowded halls in which everyone is talking at once or when someone teases or criticizes them.

Symptoms to Manage

At a recent support group meeting for kids with Tourette syndrome and their parents, a father whose ten-year-old daughter wasn't there said, "My whole family has ADHD, but my daughter is the only one with TS. She was just diagnosed a couple of months ago, and I'm still in panic mode because I don't know how bad it's going to get."

This father was reacting to the statements of two other parents who had just described their children's rages or tantrums over what seemed to be nothing. Sheryl Pruitt uses the term "Tourette storm" to describe these tornado-like outbursts. She believes that these outbursts occur when the person with TS is at the peak of overarousal and can't take any more stimuli. Stress causes a "storm" in an overaroused brain. After the outburst, the person who had it feels terrible. No wonder people who have this problem end up with low self-esteem! Many, like Caitlyn, feel helpless and hopeless.

But there is hope. We've discussed medication and psychological therapies of various kinds. But there are other things people with TS and ADHD can do at school, at home, and with friends to make their lives more comfortable and more fun.

The DSM-IV lists the symptoms of ADHD for the benefit of medical and mental health professionals who diagnose all sorts of conditions. (You may be able to find this book on the reference shelf at your public library.)

Here are some of the characteristics of a person with the inattentive type of ADHD.

⇨ Often fails to give close attention to details or makes careless mistakes in schoolwork, work, or other activities

⇨ Often has difficulty sustaining attention in tasks or play activities

⇨ Often does not seem to listen when spoken to directly

⇨ Often does not follow through on instructions and fails to finish schoolwork, chores, or duties in the workplace (not because of oppositional behavior or failure to understand instructions)

⇨ Often has difficulty organizing tasks and activities

⇨ Often avoids, dislikes, or is reluctant to engage in tasks that require sustained mental effort (such as schoolwork or homework)

⇨ Often loses things necessary for tasks or activities (for example, toys, school assignments, pencils, books, or tools)

⇨ Is often easily distracted by extraneous stimuli

⇨ Is often forgetful in daily activity

The following list indicates a person with hyperactivity.

- Often fidgets with hands or feet, or squirms in seat

- Often leaves seat in classroom or in other situations in which people are expected to remain seated

- Often runs about or climbs excessively in situations in which it is inappropriate (in adolescents or adults, may be limited to subjective feelings of restlessness)

- Often has difficulty quietly playing or engaging in leisure activities

- Is often "on the go" or often acts as if "driven by a motor"

- Often talks excessively

A young person shows impulsivity in the following ways.

- Often blurts out answers before questions have been completed

- Often has difficulty awaiting turn

- Often interrupts or intrudes on others (example, butts into conversations or games)

In order for a doctor to make a diagnosis of ADHD, the following criteria must be met.

- Symptoms present before age seven

⇝ Symptoms present for at least six months

⇝ Symptoms shown up in two different settings, such as home and school

⇝ Symptoms severe enough to cause problems

Remember that ADHD (just like tic disorders and Tourette syndrome) occurs on a continuum of severity. Not everyone will need the same coping strategies. Pick out the ones that work for you.

Action Strategies

1. Be aware of your own frustration tolerance and try not to let yourself go over the top. If you feel intense frustration coming on, the best thing is to remove yourself from the situation. Say, "Gotta go" and leave. Get a punching bag or pummel your pillow. Your family and close friends will understand and appreciate what you're doing. Others may think your behavior is a bit unusual, but most people won't consider it a big deal. Leaving is a lot better than popping someone in the nose.

   If you can't physically leave the situation, leave it mentally. Visualize a calm scene while you take six or seven deep breaths.

   If your frustration comes on more gradually—say a bad day you've managed to get through—and you're about to explode, get some exercise and/or try some of the stress relievers listed in chapter 5.

2. While making efforts to acquire new skills and abilities, also try to accept yourself and your struggles. Appreciate those struggles. Remember that you are unique; there is no one else like you. Accept the traits that make you different as part of the wonderful you.

3. Be up-front about TS and ADHD, especially with close friends and dating partners. Many people know someone who has similar symptoms. Understanding you will help them to understand their other friends and relatives. Remind them that everyone has quirks. You might have a few more than someone else.

4. Know your own special hang-ups and don't be afraid to announce them to people who don't know you well. For example, if you have attention problems, you might want to say, "Sometimes I have trouble concentrating."

5. Be a list maker. If you have OCD in addition to TS and ADHD, you may already be a list maker. Many people make to-do lists. You'll be right in style. You might even get some compliments for being organized. Shari, age sixteen, makes her list every night. She likes to type it on a five-by-eight-inch index card, which she divides into sections—before school, at school, after school. At night, she tucks her card into her backpack. The next day she enjoys crossing off the "done" items with a fat black marker. Walter, age seventeen, uses a lot of Post-it Notes as reminders. Some people prefer to use a day planner, a small notebook, or a PDA (personal digital assistant).

6. Practice problem solving. If you've always been a complete space cadet, other people, especially your parents, may have gotten into the habit of doing things for you, especially problem solving. Having someone else do your work might seem like a relief, but it's not good practice for life.

Try to start taking more responsibility for the things that affect you—for example, communicating with your teachers—and doing more effective problem solving.

The problem-solving formula is easy. First, state the problem. Second, brainstorm for solutions. (Write down everything that comes to mind.) Third, evaluate each possibility; consider the pros and cons. Fourth, pick out one solution to try. Fifth, try it. Sixth, evaluate its effectiveness. (Did it work? If yes, why? If not, why not?) Keep a strategy notebook in which you list all the tricks you're learning for solving problems. As the list grows, your confidence in your ability to solve problems will also grow. Besides that, you can refer to the list when you need to. You might want to write the problem-solving formula in your book.

Learn to take responsibility for your successes as well as your failures. (Everyone has some of each.) Write in your book what has worked and what hasn't worked. Remember to praise yourself for your successes and give twice as much weight to the successes as to the failures. (Most people do the opposite.) Some people like to write their own stories in third person. Give your "character" a name. Refer to him or her as "he" or "she." This device allows for objectivity in looking at yourself and your problems.

7. Learn more social skills. Not everyone can attend a socialization group.

   Here are some things you can practice on your own to make yourself into a person other people like to be around.

⮕ Watch your tongue. In other words, try hard not to interrupt. Almost everyone has trouble with this one. Casey says, "I interrupt because I'm interested in the conversation. I can't help it. I can't wait. I get excited!" The excitement and interest are nice, but notice how you feel when someone interrupts you midsentence. Bite your tongue or your lip to keep yourself from speaking before the other person is finished—even if that takes a long time. The other person will appreciate your patience and consider you a good listener.

⮕ Remember people's names and use them. When you meet someone new, you may be worried about how you are coming across to the other person. You forget to be interested in the other person and what he or she is saying. Show your interest by remembering the person's name. If you have trouble remembering names, write the name five times (when the person is out of sight).

⮕ Make introductions. Even if you think two people know each other, it's polite to say, "Martha, do you know Bart?" If one of the people is your mother, sure, she knows how to introduce herself. But it will be much nicer if you introduce her to the basketball coach. "Mr. Thomas (or Coach Thomas), this is my mother, Mrs. Brown." Or, "Mom, this is my coach, Mr. Thomas." Don't worry which name you say first. That's not important. The important thing is to do it.

↪ Shake hands with older people when you first meet them. If you shake hands with the new kid on the block, he'll probably think you're crazy. But shaking hands with adults when you first meet them is a gesture of respect. They'll be impressed.

↪ Practice making eye contact. Maybe you're used to looking at your shoes (or the other person's shoes) when you first meet someone new. Instead, look into his or her eyes to see what you can find there. Looking at someone with whom you're talking shows interest and helps you to understand what that person is saying. (If eye contact feels too threatening and you can't get used to doing it, you might want to explain to the person you're talking with that you are listening—even though you're not looking at him or her.)

↪ Be free with compliments. You know how good it feels when someone says something nice to you or about you. Keep in mind that other people like compliments, too. Be sincere, though. To say to someone "I like your hair" when you think it looks like a bird's nest is insincere. The person will sense you're not being honest. If you can't find something good to say, don't say anything. But you can probably find something to compliment.

⮑ Remember to say "please" and "thank you." It doesn't take much more energy to say please when you ask for something or to say thank you when someone has done something nice for you. Practice using these three little words (and don't forget "excuse me") until they become automatic.

⮑ Try to have give-and-take conversations. Think about the best conversations you've ever had. Why were they so good? Probably because they were talks in which you were so interested in what the other person was saying that you asked a lot of questions. Your new friend appreciated your interest. After he talked, he asked you a question or two, showing his interest in you. Both people talked and both people listened. Conversations with one person doing all the talking and the other person doing all the listening aren't much fun. If you don't know what kind of questions to ask a new acquaintance, try some of these: "How many different states (or cities) have you lived in?" "Do you like to travel?" "What was your best vacation?" "What do you like to do in your spare time?" "What's your sign?" "What good movies have you seen recently?" "What's your favorite sport?" "What's your favorite restaurant?" "What foods do you hate most?" "What's the most exciting thing that's ever happened to you?" If you're lucky, the other person will ask you some of the same or similar questions, which should lead to a give-and-take conversation, the most satisfying kind of talk.

↪ Don't be afraid to apologize. Everyone makes mistakes. Sometimes people fly off the handle for no apparent reason; sometimes they make false accusations or say things that hurt other people's feelings. But often people think it's a sign of weakness to apologize. It's not; apologizing is a sign of strength. Can you remember a time one of your parents apologized for yelling at you or blaming you for something that wasn't your fault? How did this apology make you feel? Of course, apologizing is not an excuse for constant wrongdoing. But a sincere apology for a thoughtless action goes a long way.

↪ In any relationship, don't play games. Almost always, honesty is the best policy. This includes honesty about your particular medical condition. You don't have to "tell all" though. A little explanation can go a long way. For example, if your particular type of TS or ADHD causes you to be hyper, you might say, "Sometimes I get really wound up." It isn't as if your friends haven't already noticed that.

8. Take an inventory of your social skills and work on deficiencies. Start out with a list of positives and then go on to skills you need to work on.

My good points:

↪ Usually polite; for example, saying "please" and "thank you"

↪ Table manners not too horrible

↪ Usually arrive on time for appointments

Things I need to work on:

- Listening carefully and not interrupting when someone is talking

- Learning to start a conversation with someone I don't know

- Being able to ask someone out

- Asking for help when I need it

- Offering to help other people

- Settling disagreements with talk, not force

- Starting to invite people over

Action Strategies for Learning

At School

One of the most important skills for success at home and at school is the ability to solve problems. Now let's apply the problem-solving process to a school-related problem.

- State the problem. What exactly is bugging you? Is it your problem to solve? Try to state the problem in one sentence. For example, Scott said, "I'm flunking out of school because I haven't been turning in homework assignments."

☞ Review possible solutions. Scott decided he could do one of the following.

1. Drop out of school and get his GED.

2. Change schools and get into an easier one.

3. Break the TV, so he wouldn't watch it so much.

4. Stop talking on the telephone.

5. Start his homework immediately after school (and take the telephone off the hook for sixty minutes).

☞ Evaluate each possibility.

☞ Choose the best solution. Scott decided to try the right-after-school approach to homework.

☞ List the reason this choice appears to be the best. Do it! This step was easy because the rest of the alternatives were pretty silly. The hardest part would be doing it.

☞ Look back and decide whether the chosen solution really was the best. Why? Why not? Six weeks after Scott started doing his homework right after school, his grades had gone up to three Bs and two Cs. He had modified his plan a bit. Because of his hyperactivity and restlessness, he needed at least two separate sessions to get the work done. (This was the first time Scott had ever taken a look at his ADHD symptoms.) Now he does half of his homework right after school and the other half right after dinner.

The action strategies that follow will be useful no matter what type of school you attend—high school, vocational school, or college. Use some of them and make up some of your own.

⮕ If your parents want to get you a tutor for a particular subject, don't fight them. A tutor can be a support and a friend, as well as a helper.

⮕ Whenever possible, choose classes with small-group discussions and experiential (hands-on) learning.

⮕ Whenever possible, use a laptop computer for taking notes. If it's not possible and you have trouble with notetaking, see whether you can arrange (with your instructor's permission) for someone else to take notes and give you a copy. You might want to ask your teacher to assign you a buddy—someone who volunteers for the job. Ask if you can help choose this person.

⮕ Arrange to take untimed tests. If you're not in a race to the finish line, you'll have less test anxiety and do much better overall.

⮕ Whenever possible, try for preferential seating. You might feel that sitting at the front of the room gives you unwanted visibility and is therefore out of the question. But you might be able to get a seat off to the side, which will help you to concentrate and filter out distractions. It will also give you quick access to the door in case you need to take prearranged breaks.

⮕ Squeezing a small rubber ball or an eraser can relieve tension. Likewise, chewing gum (again with

106

the teacher's permission) can help to reduce some of the stress associated with tics and ADHD.

⮑ Keep in your locker or some other safe place an extra supply of pencils, pens, paper, and notebooks. Use them for emergencies, such as the times you space out and leave these supplies at home, on the bus, or in your friend's car.

⮑ If you're not worried about seeming different, you might try leaving one or more classes a couple of minutes early so you'll have the opportunity to compose yourself at your locker before the horde of other students descends.

⮑ If possible, arrange for someone to help you clean out your backpack, desk, notebook or notebooks, and locker once a week.

At Home
Here are some tips to help get assignments done efficiently and on time.

⮑ Before you leave a class for the day, have the teacher, instructor, or an aide check your assignment book to make certain the information and dates are correct.

⮑ Realize and accept your need for structure. Structure means having a set time to do homework, making written schedules of what to do when, and doing homework in the same quiet place every day. When you go to that place, it should say, "Study here."

➥ Keep the supplies you'll need—pencils, pens, notebooks, paper, a timer—in a box in your study place. Some people even keep an extra set of textbooks at home.

➥ If possible, use a word processor for your assignments. In *Teaching the Tiger*, Dornbush and Pruitt say that 90 percent of young people with TS and ADHD have handwriting problems. Just as most people with muscular dystrophy make use of a wheelchair, say these experts, those with Tourette syndrome and/or ADHD need a computer, word processor, and printer.

➥ Prioritize. Think: What is the most important thing I have to do tonight? Second? Third? Then do your assignments in that order.

➥ Break down big assignments into smaller sections. Set short-term goals. Finish one small section before you start the next one. Otherwise the whole thing may look so overwhelming, you'll never get started—not to mention getting finished.

➥ After you reach a short-term goal, take a break. Set your timer so the break doesn't last all night. Five minutes? Ten?

➥ Plan a reward for yourself during your break or do a different kind of activity, something that doesn't use too much brainpower. Eat an apple. Make one quick call to a friend. Get a shoulder massage from a family member.

➥ Some people like to wear a headset that plays soft music (or their favorite kind of music). For some people, music screens out distractions and helps them concentrate.

↪ With the goal of improving your reading, do some pleasure reading (magazines, newspapers, comic books) at home. Start with fifteen minutes, stretch that to thirty, then work up to sixty minutes each day.

↪ As soon as you finish a homework assignment, put it in its place. Use the same place every day. Some people like to color-code various sections of a notebook. For example, put a red cover on your math book, use a red notebook for math, and put your math homework in a red folder.

↪ Get everything, including homework assignments, ready for school the night before. As you leave in the morning, recheck (using a list, if necessary) to make sure you have everything you need.

Be patient with yourself. The older you get, the wiser you'll get. The farther along you get in school, the better you'll become at using the action strategies that work best for you. Give yourself a pat on the back. Emphasize the positive. You're doing a great job.

Strategies for Coping with Tourette Syndrome (Plus Obsessive-Compulsive Disorder)

No one knows exactly how many people with Tourette syndrome also have obsessive-compulsive behaviors (or disorder). Estimates range from 30 to 90 percent. The true extent of the problem is unknown because most people try to keep their obsessive thoughts and compulsive behaviors hidden. Trying to control tics while also trying to control obsessions and compulsions takes a tremendous amount of energy. No wonder people with obsessive-compulsive behaviors in addition to TS try to keep their secret. If friends and relatives find out, what will they think? "Most people think I'm already weird enough," says Louis, age sixteen. "If they find out I have OCD, on top of tics, they'll start running." These kinds of worries may cause people with TS and OCD to withdraw from the company of other people. They might be afraid to let anyone get close.

Experts think that about 2.5 percent of all adults have OCD. Genetic studies show that obsessions and compulsions run in families just like Tourette syndrome. In fact, many geneticists believe both conditions are alternative expressions of the same genetic predisposition or tendency.

Some rituals and superstitions, obsessions, and compulsions are normal. Most people occasionally have the urge to go back into the house to see if they locked a door or turned off the iron. Most people have knocked on wood for good luck or avoided a black cat crossing their path. These people may have obsessive-compulsive traits or features. According to the DSM-IV, however, in order to have true OCD, people must have obsessions or compulsions that severely disrupt their lives.

Let's say you're a person who has obsessive thoughts or compulsive behaviors (or both) that mess you up big time. Is there hope for you? Of course. Medications for obsessions and compulsions (discussed in chapter 3) can greatly help. In addition, psychologists who specialize in treating obsessions and compulsions often use a cognitive-behavioral approach to treat OCD. Cognitive and behavioral therapies are close cousins. They both focus on changing the thinking that causes us to act as we do. In dealing with obsessions and compulsions, some therapists suggest accepting the obsessive thoughts instead of fighting them. Practice your affirmations (discussed in chapter 5) and gear them toward acceptance. For example, you could repeat the following several times: "These obsessions are just thoughts. They won't kill me." Or "Obsessions are part of the unique me." As amazing as it seems, your acceptance can be the first step in calming these pesky thoughts.

Another technique that works for some people is postponing the obsession or compulsion for several minutes, an hour, or even longer until it disappears. Another way to get rid of obsessions and compulsions is to get away from them by immersing yourself in something else. In other words, get a new and healthier compulsion—a hobby, for example.

Here are some more ideas.

⇝ Relax. Calm down. Slow down. Stop and smell the flowers—or the movie-theater popcorn. People with obsessions and compulsions often feel uptight and stressed out.

⇝ Get out of your mind and into your body. Our old friend exercise will help. You can also try the relaxation exercises described in detail in chapter 5—progressive muscle relaxation, yoga, tai chi, meditation, breathing exercises, visualization, and imagery.

⇝ Pay attention to your self-talk. Eliminate obsessive "shoulds." For example, if you're tempted to go inside and check the stove burners for the second time, don't say to yourself, "I should check the burners." Instead say, "No. I checked the burners once, and they were turned off." Then leave.

⇝ Try controlling your thoughts rather than letting your thoughts control you. Writing your thoughts, feelings, and tasks on paper can help. Try daily journal writing. Don't say, "I should write in my journal." Just do it whenever you think of it.

⇝ Get out with people. If you "live in your head" most of the time, no wonder you're obsessing. Besides that, you may be getting rather boring. Get out of the house and out of your head. Find someone else to get interested in.

⇝ Redirect yourself. Don't stay with something you know is getting you nowhere (for example, obsessions and compulsions). Try to direct yourself to a different activity. Steve lost interest in piano lessons at age seven. Now at sixteen, he wants to try again. He thought practicing would be much easier this time. It wasn't. As Steve compulsively banged on the piano keys, he became more frustrated with his inability to produce the beautiful music he expected. So, he went upstairs and banged on his brother's drum set. Steve found that playing the drums released tension. Now his parents have two drummers in the family.

⇨ If you have trouble deciding what to wear in the morning and you're obsessing about a certain shirt that feels scratchy, you are going to be late. Instead of going through this agonizing routine every morning, lay out your clothes at night. Put them on in the morning and do not change them under any circumstances.

The story on OCD is not completely downbeat. People with obsessions and compulsions are often well organized and stick with tasks that other people would give up on. Also, studies show that OCD improves with age. Of patients studied for forty years in Sweden, 48 percent had completely recovered and a total of 83 percent showed at least some improvement.

But people with Tourette syndrome and the associated conditions of ADHD and OCD get a triple whammy. If so-called normal people show little tolerance for tics, add symptoms of ADHD and OCD and see what happens. You will have to draw on inner strength and outside support to show others that you are much more than the sum of your characteristics.

Strategies for Coping with Tourette Syndrome (Plus Learning Differences)

Learning differences (sometimes called learning disabilities or learning disorders) often go along with Tourette syndrome and attention disorders. Most experts agree that up to 60 percent of young people with TS have problems with learning although they have average or above average intelligence. Many of these young people—maybe 50 percent—have severe learning disabilities. Boys with LD outnumber girls three to one. There is no medical cure, such as medication, for LD.

What Does the Term "Learning Differences" Mean?

The term "learning differences" describes a person's inability to figure out exactly what he or she is seeing or hearing. Or it may refer to a person's inability to link information in various parts of the brain. Your first clue may be that you're not doing well in certain school subjects even though you try hard and know you're smart. You may have trouble organizing your work or your time; you may have difficulty remembering facts you thought you knew; you may not be able to memorize a speech or a piece of music; you may have a problem understanding written or spoken directions; you may have trouble expressing yourself in speaking, writing, or both; you may have difficulty with spelling, writing, reading, math, or all of the above. Having a learning disability does not mean the inability to learn. Instead, the person with LD learns in different ways.

One thing you might want to try to figure out is your own learning style, sometimes called your learning preference. Everyone has certain ways they learn best. Many people are experiential learners; they learn best by doing or experiencing something. Some people are auditory language learners. These people learn better through what they hear. An example is a child who learns to read with phonics (or sounding words out). Other people are visual learners. They learn more quickly if they see written words. As children, these people may have learned to read using sight-reading or a so-called whole language approach to reading. At age seventeen, Sierra, a visual learner, is trying hard to remember people's names after she has met them once. When she meets someone for the first time, she repeats the name in her head until she can write it down. Then she takes a long look at what she has written, which helps her to remember.

It's often difficult to tell the difference between ADHD and LD. Some people call ADHD a kind of learning disability. Sorting a person's learning differences into categories is like trying to unravel a ball of yarn that is glued together—it's an impossible job.

Jake's handwriting frustrates him and anyone else who tries to read it. No matter how hard he tries, the words he writes are small and shaky-looking, as if he wrote them while riding on a motorcycle. Usually when he writes, Jake tries to hurry because he knows his tics are slowing him down. But one professional who tested him said that Jake might have ADHD because he tends to rush through most of his schoolwork. A doctor said Jake had dysgraphia, which means trouble with writing and fine motor activities.

Another "dys" word frequently used with LD is dyslexia. Originally, dyslexia described a condition in which an older child or adult reversed certain letters such as *b* and *d* or numbers such as 6 and 9. Nowadays, the word "dyslexia" is used to describe any reading disability and is sometimes used incorrectly to describe any learning disability.

Causes of Learning Differences

The causes of LD are, in many cases, similar to the causes of TS and ADHD. Learning disabilities seem to run in families, which means that heredity probably plays a part.

Just as there are different ways of categorizing Tourette syndrome, there are various ways of categorizing learning disorders.

We can categorize LD two ways: by what comes into the brain through the five senses, such as hearing and seeing (incoming disabilities), and by what goes out from the brain (outgoing disabilities).

Incoming Disabilities

Problems absorbing incoming information include visual perceptual problems, auditory perceptual problems, problems with time, sequencing problems, difficulty with spatial relationships, and memory problems.

↪ You may have 20/20 vision but still have visual perception problems, or making sense of what you see. Dyslexia (recognizing letters and numbers, mentioned earlier) is one example. Finding "hidden pictures" or doing jigsaw puzzles may not be your thing. You may have trouble distinguishing the facial expressions or facial characteristics of different people.

↪ If you have problems with auditory processing, your hearing is probably fine. But you have various kinds of difficulty with the spoken word. In a lecture class, you may take longer than your friends to figure out what your instructor means. In a discussion group, you're usually silent because you can't grasp fast enough what others are saying. You might tune out or ask people to repeat what they just said. Sometimes your answer to a question makes people laugh. Or they tease you because your answer didn't have anything to do with the question.

↪ Difficulties with the concept of time may mean that you're always late or that your assignments are often late because you miscalculate the time needed to get things done. An alarm clock or alarm watch may help with the first problem. For the second problem, sketch out timelines that tell you exactly what needs to be done by what time to accomplish the whole project.

↪ Sequencing difficulties may involve problems with planning or deciding what to do first (prioritizing). You might have trouble making and sticking to schedules. If someone gives you several directions at once, you may have trouble carrying through. If your mom says, "Please hang up your coat and then tell Dad to come in for dinner," you may remember only to hang up your coat.

↪ Difficulties with spatial relationships include problems centering yourself in space. For example, you may have trouble driving a car because you can't figure out how close you are to the other cars. Or people call you clumsy because you're always bumping into things or knocking things over. If you have problems with spatial relationships, you probably won't be a gymnast, platform diver, or trapeze artist.

↪ People with memory problems have trouble learning things by rote. They won't be standing in front of the class reciting the Gettysburg Address. They might also have deficits in their short-term memory, such as forgetting what they had for lunch, the name of the person they met an hour ago, or what they wanted to get when they went upstairs. Those with long-term memory problems have trouble recalling information for tests, what happened two summers ago, or the state in which their grandparents live.

Outgoing Disabilities
Outgoing disabilities involve problems with the processing of information that comes out of your mouth and into the world at large. You might have trouble with the production and expression of information. For example, you may not be able to say exactly what you're thinking

or write what you'd like to write. You may have trouble telling stories or jokes.

Areas Affected by Learning Disabilities

Another way of categorizing learning disabilities is by the academic subject area they affect—such as reading, writing, and math.

Reading Difficulties (Dyslexia)

Reading is a complex skill. Think how many activities go into reading this paragraph. You need to recognize individual letters and the sounds that go with them. Your eyes must focus on the letters and words, and then scroll across the page. You must recognize punctuation marks and obey them. Your brain must make images related to the words. In your mind, you need to relate these images to other images stored in your brain. When you read aloud, you need to pronounce the words so others will understand them.

Writing Difficulties (Dysgraphia)

Writing is another complex activity, which not only involves forming the letters, but also demands that you put words together in meaningful sentences and paragraphs. Many people with learning disabilities (as well as people without LD) have problems with spelling. (Look at the word "writing." What is that "w" doing in front of the "r"?) Good spellers are often good readers. So if reading is hard for you, spelling may also be difficult. Good spellers need to be able to hear the word pronounced correctly, which may not be possible if you have auditory processing problems. People with dysgraphia may have shaky-looking or messy handwriting. They may also have trouble writing on the lines or may be unable to write without lines. (Words on their pages may look like runaway roller coasters.) They may have trouble using correct punctuation marks, such as commas and periods. Writing also involves the ability to organize chunks of information.

Math Difficulties (Dyscalculia)

Doing math is another complex activity. People who reverse their numbers (for example, writing 25 instead of 52) are in trouble from the start. Putting numbers in straight rows with decimal points in the right places can also be impossible for some people. What about memorizing the multiplication tables? And think how many different steps are necessary to figure out three-fourths of twenty-six.

Action Strategies for Learning Disabilities

Many of the action strategies (coping techniques) that work for ADHD will also work with LD. Here are a few extra suggestions for specific subject areas.

If you have reading difficulties, get creative.

- ⮧ Borrow some books on tape from the public library or get a videotape to give you an idea of the characters and plot of a story, or use published book summaries, such as Cliffs Notes. You might also be eligible to borrow taped texts from the Library of Congress (National Library Service for the Blind and Physically Handicapped; call (202) 707-5100 for more information).

➥ Try reading portions of a book or story aloud. Tape-record your reading. Playing back your tape will help to fix the details in your mind. The reading itself will be good practice. One of the best ways to improve your reading is to read.

➥ Outlining or taking notes on what you're reading may help with remembering.

➥ If you have trouble keeping your place when reading, use a ruler or bookmark as you go down the page. Some people use a highlighter to emphasize important sections.

➥ Become friends with your school media specialist or local public librarian. These people may know of computer aids and other learning aids the rest of the world hasn't yet heard about.

If you have writing and/or spelling difficulties, try the following.

➥ Use a word processor or a laptop at school whenever possible. Be sure to use the spell check and grammar check.

➥ When you write, use all the resources at your disposal, such as printing instead of cursive writing, rubber grips on your pencils, and lined or graph paper. Some people have found that working with an occupational therapist helps.

➥ Learn how to outline so that you can break your thoughts into small, manageable segments.

If you have problems with math, try the following.

- ⇨ It's OK to use your fingers (and toes) for counting, if you need to.

- ⇨ Always carry a calculator. Use it to check your answers. (Be sure to use the calculator only as a backup, not as a substitute for learning math concepts.)

- ⇨ Flash cards and math fact charts can help with the learning of multiplication tables and other quick math facts, such as 4 + 8. You can use a calculator for this purpose, too.

- ⇨ Graph paper helps some people get used to the proper way to space numbers.

- ⇨ If you have difficulty writing numbers, such as those you might need to write on a check, carry these written names with the corresponding numeral on a card in your wallet. Thirteen=13, twenty=20, and so on.

- ⇨ If you have problems with multiple-step math problems, do each step on a different line. Don't try to skip steps.

- ⇨ Draw pictures or make pictures in your head to help with word problems.

If you're a person with LD, you might need to work harder than others at finding your own best ways of learning.

Many young people with TS also have behavior problems. If you do, the most important thing to remember is that you are not your behavior any more than you are your

Tourette syndrome. Your behavior might not be good (it may even be horrible at times), but you are not an evil or bad person. However, substandard behavior does not mean you shouldn't have to face the consequences of your behavior. Learning the hard way is the only way some people learn.

Strategies for Coping with Tourette Syndrome (Plus Behavior Problems)

At age fourteen, Nick took his parents' car for a joyride. When he brought it back, the blue sedan had two flat tires and a smashed fender. His mom discovered the damage the next day when Nick was at school. At age fifteen, Nick "borrowed" the car again without his parents' knowledge to drive to a basketball practice. His parents went to the school to confront him and to get the keys. At sixteen without a license, Nick drove a friend's car. A police officer picked him up for speeding.

When Nick stole money from his mother's purse, she decided to keep her purse in a locked closet. Nick took the door off its hinges. In his senior year, his school expelled him for stealing money from other students. Nick's parents warned him that when he turned eighteen, he would need to find another place to live and they would no longer take responsibility for him.

Family counseling didn't seem to help; Nick could never admit his part in family conflicts. He blamed Tourette syndrome, ADHD, or whatever came to mind. The day after Nick's eighteenth birthday, his parents asked him if he would like to go with them to pick out his room at the YMCA. He said he couldn't; he was going fishing. His parents gave him a $500 check, packed up his belongings, took them to the YMCA, and paid for a room for Nick for a month. Nick stayed one night. He said it was too noisy and *he didn't like the "characters" who stayed there. He went to live with friends.*

Nick lost his supermarket job for shoplifting; he quit other jobs after only a week. Before three months had passed, Nick was living on the streets.

Eventually he found his way to a shelter for homeless and runaway teens. After getting his GED, Nick accepted help from the social worker at the shelter, who helped him get into the local community college. However, he didn't do the work and flunked out.

By this time, Nick had a credit card, a cell phone, and lots of bills, which he couldn't pay. He decided to move to another state to live with a friend.

Nick is turning twenty next month. His parents have already sent him an early birthday present so he can pay the damage deposit on a new apartment. They sent him a shirt for his birthday, but they're wondering if he'll get it.

A bigger question is, "Will he ever get it?" They mean, will Nick ever understand that his actions have consequences? Will he ever learn? They hope so.

For whatever reasons, some young people make poor decisions and wrong choices. These behavior problems usually fall into the following categories: problems related to driving a car; smoking, drinking, and/or using illegal drugs; problems related to sex; and problems with the law.

Smoking, Drinking, and Drugs

How many of your friends smoke, drink alcohol, or use illegal drugs? One of the main predictors of your use of these substances is your friends. You've heard this advice before: If you don't smoke, drink, or use drugs, don't start.

But everybody's doing it! Actually, some are and some aren't. However, if you look at those who are abusing substances the most, you will see people with low self-esteem who don't feel as if they have enough other resources to help them cope with life.

Do you have Tourette syndrome? Do you have an associated condition such as ADHD or OCD? If so, you may think (consciously or unconsciously) that you need a crutch, something to lean on. You probably do. Everybody does. But the use of nicotine, alcohol, or illegal drugs to numb out, to help dull hurt feelings, or to keep people from getting to you only adds problems on top of problems.

The good news for those who feel as if they've gotten in over their heads is that help is everywhere. You might want to start by asking your doctor for resources or by looking up Alcoholics Anonymous, Nicotine Anonymous, or Narcotics Anonymous in the telephone book. If you become involved with these organizations and groups similar to them, you'll find that support comes from people who have been in similar situations, that you don't need addictive substances as a crutch, and that you don't have to go through life alone.

Sexual Issues

Most young people dream of being intimate with another person. Intimacy means different things. It may mean sharing your deepest thoughts and feelings with another person. Many people with Tourette syndrome wonder whether an intimate relationship will ever be possible for them.

Tim, age eighteen, says, "I've never even had a date. It would take more guts than I've got to assume a girl would want to be around my tics for even one night not to mention for a longer period or a long-term relationship."

In spite of what Tim says, people with TS get married, have kids, and have long and fulfilling relationships. According to one marital therapist, "If Mary and John get married, and John has Tourette syndrome, you can be pretty sure Mary is looking past superficial things such as tics to the wonderful human being John is."

Intimacy can also mean sexual intimacy, and this is where young people sometimes get into trouble. If you're a person who has TS and associated ADHD, you might have the characteristic of impulsivity (acting before you think) that causes you to get in over your head. In addition, if you've been drinking, your defenses come tumbling down, and you may take risks you normally wouldn't take. Sexual urges are strong during the teen years. That is why it's important to think ahead of time to consider various scenarios.

First, remember that it's OK to say no. In fact, at your age it's best to say no. If a friend (or a date) is pressuring you to get sexually active before you're ready, have your answers ready. Early in a relationship, you can set the ground rules by saying something like this: "I like going out with you. We have a good time, but I'm not into any physical stuff." If you're feeling pressured, there are many other things you can say.

- ➯ "No thanks. I don't see a baby in my immediate future."

- ➯ "Everyone is not doing it, and I plan to stay in the inactive group."

127

➤ "I don't believe in sex before marriage, and marriage isn't in my plans right now."

➤ "My mother says I'm too young for sex."

But seriously, there is a lot of advice and support out there for teens who need help with navigating the world of love and relationships. There are some books listed in the For Further Reading section of this book that can help you.

Problems with the Law/Problems with Life

Some people have a knack for getting into trouble. One thing leads to the next, and before long, the person can't seem to get out of the pit. This sinking feeling causes a sense of helplessness that leads to depression.

Many young people report that if they had stopped to think of the possible consequences of their actions, they wouldn't have done what they did. Below are a few of these actions.

➤ Driving without a license

➤ Driving under the influence of alcohol or drugs

➤ Speeding

➤ Driving without insurance

➤ Getting stopped by the police for being out after curfew

➤ Giving a false name when stopped by the police

➯ Arguing with a police officer

➯ Shoplifting

➯ Stealing from other people

➯ Stealing from other people's homes

➯ Getting a girl pregnant

➯ Getting pregnant

➯ Getting a sexually transmitted disease

➯ Carrying a knife or gun to school

➯ Using illegal drugs

➯ Spraying graffiti or committing other acts of vandalism

➯ Getting into fights in which someone gets hurt

Nobody's perfect. No one is asking you to be perfect. But as you get older, you may start to realize that it's in your own best interest to keep out of trouble. Having support—in psychotherapy or group counseling—can be a great tool to help you strategize ways to put your positive energy to work.

Strategies for Coping with Tourette Syndrome (Plus Sleep Difficulties)

People with Tourette syndrome often have problems with sleep. Not getting enough sleep can start a vicious cycle because tics sometimes increase when sleep decreases. The following tips will help you get your shut-eye.

- Remember the benefits of exercise? Exercise at any time of the day, except right before bedtime, will make you tired and help you to sleep. Get at least thirty minutes of aerobic exercise every day.

- Try to resist taking naps. Naps interrupt the normal sleep cycle. If you're tempted to take a nap after school or after dinner, splash some cold water on your face or go walk the dog. Don't give into it.

- As much as possible, go to bed at the same time every night and get up at the same time every morning. No matter how cruel this advice sounds, don't sleep in—even on weekends.

- In the evening, avoid big meals and caffeinated drinks. Remember that caffeine lurks in hot chocolate, chocolate candy, soft drinks, some teas, and coffee. If you can, check the label of what you're drinking.

Even decaf coffee has some caffeine. In the evening stick to water or fruit juices.

☞ Don't smoke. Nicotine is a stimulant just like caffeine.

☞ Try to wind down before going to bed. Avoid scary TV programs, horror movies, and depressing books. Play some soft music or relaxation tapes.

☞ If noise is a problem, get some earplugs or try one of the new machines that produces soothing sounds. A humming electric fan works wonders for some people.

☞ If you can't sleep, don't force it and don't worry about it. Counting sheep may help, but if nothing works after thirty minutes, get up and have a cup of warm milk (grandma's remedy) or a cup of herbal tea. Or get up and read until you feel sleepy.

☞ Try to keep your bedroom at a comfortable temperature. Too hot or too cold can keep you awake.

☞ Make a before-bedtime ritual for yourself. A warm bath works for some people.

☞ Work on achieving a clear conscience. If you've done or said something hurtful to another person during the day, your conscience may bother you at night when you're trying to sleep. Take a tip from the various twelve-step recovery programs. Make amends. Not only do you need to apologize to the person you've harmed, but you also need to do something to make up for the wrongdoing. One day in anger, Jocelyn called her friend Toya "stupid." Toya left the scene in tears. That night the argument kept replaying in Jocelyn's head. She couldn't sleep until she promised herself she would apologize to Toya the next day.

↪ Visualize a pleasant, relaxing scene and put yourself in the middle of that picture. Don't make the action too exciting, though, or it will keep you awake.

↪ If you're up half the night, you may have trouble waking up in the morning. Set at least two alarm clocks or alarm clock radios, one close to your bed and one far enough away that you have to get up to turn it off (but not so far away that you can't hear it).

No doubt you'll find your own sleep remedies to add to the list.

Laws That Can Help You

Your Education

Various types of laws and regulations affect your education. Because it's your education, you'll want to be able to advocate for yourself whenever possible. Learning something about these laws is important.

If you find these laws too complicated, you and your parents may decide to hire an educational consultant. For information and/or referrals, call your local Tourette Syndrome Association or talk to people in your TS support group.

Federal (national) laws are, of course, the same for people in every state. Usually federal laws establish minimum standards for special education, or "special ed." Some people resist this label. That's fine; some people don't need extra help. But if you need it because you have TS, you should get some idea about what is available under the laws.

One important federal law is the Rehabilitation Act of 1973, also called PL 93-112. This law protects individuals with a handicapping condition from being discriminated against. Especially important is section 504, which provides for special physical accommodations. The law applies to agencies that receive federal funding, including school districts.

A second important federal law is the Individuals with Disabilities Education Act (IDEA). Approximately every four years, Congress makes changes and reauthorizes

IDEA. Originally called PL 94-142, or the Education for All Handicapped Children Act of 1975 (EAHCA), the law requires public schools to provide a free, appropriate education to all young people with disabilities in the least restrictive environment. Also, parents of a person with a disability such as TS can request in writing an Individualized Education Plan (IEP). The school usually has thirty days to set the wheels in motion (for example, giving a series of tests, such as the Conners Teacher Rating Scale, or CTRS). If it is determined that the student is in need of special services, a team will develop an IEP. Those who make up the evaluation-decision team include you and your parents, a regular education teacher, a special-ed teacher, and various other school personnel, such as a psychologist, social worker, nurse, and/or school administrator.

Within thirty days after the completion of testing, you and your parents should be notified in writing about a meeting to discuss results and the IEP. You might want to arrange to bring a representative from the local Tourette Syndrome Association or your educational consultant to the meeting.

After discussing the plan (short-term and long-term goals), you and your parents will probably decide to sign it. If after much discussion you don't agree with the plan, you don't have to sign it. You can find out about procedures for appeal from your local Tourette Syndrome Association. If you agree with the plan, you should immediately start to receive the agreed-upon services. If the school can't meet your needs, then the district must find an alternative public or private school to give the needed services.

The team reviews the IEP every year and makes the needed changes.

Other Laws

In 1990, Congress passed the Americans with Disabilities Act (ADA), also called PL 101-336, designed to wipe out discrimination against people with disabilities in all areas of life, not only in education or in federally funded programs. This law protects people with Tourette syndrome from job discrimination and other discrimination. Employers must make reasonable accommodations to help people with TS to do their jobs. The employer cannot consider learning disabilities as a reason not to hire someone.

The Developmental Disabilities Act of 1978 helps young people with Tourette syndrome who have severe disabilities. This act provides for a protection and advocacy office in every state as well as case management services for those who need this help. Services such as respite workers and in-home aides might be covered.

If you immerse yourself in it, a study of local and federal laws can be fascinating. Anyone who understands these laws is certain to be in demand.

Planning for the Future

No matter what your dreams are, now is the time to start getting real about the future—your future. It's not too early to start considering that one of these days you're going to be on your own.

Work? Technical school? Community college? Four-year university? Some people have no choice. They must go to work. Others do have a choice; they want to go to college. But for some young people the idea of college has nothing to do with career goals. They want to go to college because it sounds like fun, their parents will pay for it, and all their friends are going. Finally, they can get away from home!

If you've had similar thoughts, stop and ask yourself this question: Is college right for me? Maybe. Maybe not. But don't let anyone say you can't do it. If you have Tourette syndrome with or without ADHD, you can go to college. Take some time to consider and evaluate your motives. Ask yourself questions like the following.

➷ Do I like reading, writing, studying, and learning?

➷ Can I do the work?

➷ How will college prepare me for a career?

Is vocational counseling available at your school? If so, make use of it. See if you can get some books from the library, such as the *Occupational Outlook Handbook, The*

Big Book of Jobs, or *What Color Is Your Parachute?* Maybe you can arrange to take an interest or aptitude test, such as the Meyers-Briggs Type Indicator that classifies your personality type and what kind of job you might do best.

Don't underestimate the value of volunteer work for getting a first-hand look at various occupations. For example, if you volunteer to read to a person in a nursing home, you can observe aides and orderlies, nurses and doctors, custodians and food service personnel, as well as dieticians and occupational and physical therapists.

"Shadowing" is another way of getting a look at certain careers. When Chuck said he wanted to go to college and major in engineering, his dad begged him to make an appointment to spend the day with an electrical engineer, a friend of the family. Chuck didn't want his dad to set anything up for him, but never got around to making the appointment himself. He got into an engineering school where he lasted one semester. "What am I doing here?" he asked himself. "I don't have an engineer's mind. This isn't for me."

If you have Tourette syndrome, ADHD, or LD, you may need to do more thinking than the average person about what you're going to do after high school. Some people look at colleges that specialize in offering services to those with different learning styles. Even if you're tired of the LD label and want to shake it, you'd be smart to consider a school that at least offers some special services—even if you don't plan to use them.

College Admission: Questions to Ask

Asking questions like the following may help you to find the school that is perfect for you.

☞ What kind of support services does the school have for students with TS, ADHD, OCD, or LD?

☞ How big are the classes?

☞ Is tutoring available for students with LD? Is it included in the tuition? If not, how much does a tutor cost?

☞ Are there rigid math and foreign language requirements?

☞ Can students substitute some courses for others?

☞ Is a thesis or senior project required for graduation?

Be up-front with the people in the admissions office. If they don't know your needs, how can they help you? Similarly, when you get ready to apply for college, find out about special arrangements, such as untimed tests. Your counselor or therapist will help with documentation for you to take the ACT (American College Testing Assessment) or SAT (Scholastic Aptitude Test) without rigid time restrictions.

Don't wait until the last minute to consider these suggestions. If you do, you may be waving good-bye as your friends go off to various exciting destinations while you sit at home.

Other Things to Consider

As you get older, no matter what your post–high school choices, you're going to want more independence. It's never too early to start thinking about the greater responsibilities of maturity. (Sounds pretty heavy, doesn't it?) One of the most important things to think about is money management.

Financial Matters

Most parents would love to help their children become financially responsible. Most young people don't want this help. However, if you hope to live on your own soon, if you have a job and would like to save some money, if you want to have your own checking account or credit card, or if you don't know a thing about budgeting, now is the time to start learning. Talk to people with experience.

Budgeting

Maybe your parents would be willing to show you where their monthly income goes. Here are some basic categories: housing, food, utilities (gas, electric, water), telephone, transportation, entertainment, savings, and miscellaneous. If you're going to college, your parents may pay for your room and board and plan to give you a living allowance. But eventually you're going to have to make house payments or pay rent. Ask your parents what percentage of their monthly income goes to housing. What percentage of their monthly income do they spend on food? If you get your clothes at the thrift store, you'll have money left over for other things. Prioritize. Do you want new clothes or cable TV? What about your phone service? Do you need voice messaging, call forwarding, call waiting, and a pager? Or would you rather spend more money on entertainment items, such as eating out and going to movies?

Banking and Cash-Flow Issues

If you have a part-time job and haven't already opened a checking account, now is the time. Learn to write checks and keep a record. Subtract the amount of the check from your total and keep a balance. Learn how to use an ATM (automatic teller machine) and a debit card. Remember that checks take a day or two to clear at the bank.

Some people like to put a certain amount of each check into a savings account before they cash their check and start spending. In this way, they build for the future; they also have a cushion for any overspending. A credit card can be a major convenience or a major headache.

Sylvie, age nineteen, had graduated from high school, gotten her first real job, and moved into her own apartment. She felt flattered to receive so many credit cards she hadn't even asked for. She used them all. Soon Sylvie had $3,000 worth of bills she couldn't pay.

Be sure you have a chunk of money in the bank or a steady job before you use a credit card—unless, of course, your parents are willing to pay for any charges you rack up.

Independent Living

Other matters you might want to consider before moving into the world include where to live, the question of room-mates, household skills, and transportation issues.

Where to Live

The place you pick will depend, to a large extent, on your financial situation and your transportation. If you don't have a car, you may want to live close to school or work— or at least close to a bus line.

The Question of Roommates

Again, one thing depends on something else. If you're a person with certain habits related to TS, ADHD, and/or OCD, you may decide to live alone. If you have trouble getting along with other people or think your tics might bother them, a roommate or roommates may not work well for you. On the other hand, each roommate you have makes the rent that much cheaper. Also, if you have a tendency toward depression, a roommate (a living, breathing person hanging around) might lift your spirits. But BEWARE. Get everything down in writing before you move in or let a roommate move in. Don't take full responsibility for household accounts. You might get stuck with some unwanted and unexpected bills.

Becca was eighteen when she moved into an apartment with two other girls. She didn't know her two new housemates well and wanted them to like her. So when they suggested she put the telephone and utility bill in her name, she agreed. Three months later, they both moved out, and Becca was stuck with their bills, which included several long-distance phone calls.

Household Skills

Be sure to divide household responsibilities from the beginning. No one wants to be the sole in-house toilet-bowl cleaner. In addition, you might want to ask yourself the following questions.

→ What can I cook? Is it good to live on candy bars, fast food, and soda? Do I know the basic food

141

safety rules, like keep hot foods hot and cold foods cold?

⮑ Do I know how to do laundry?

⮑ Have I ever cleaned a bathroom (that is, toilet, sink, floor, mirror)?

⮑ Have I ever cleaned up a kitchen?

Transportation Issues

Another basic issue is whether you will have a car. No young person wants to hear this, but if you're earning your own money, you'll be better off without one. Most colleges issue inexpensive bus passes. Taking public transportation forces you to get some exercise, and it relieves you of many expenses. Be sure to consider the following before you invest in a car: car payments, insurance premiums (which may rise to excruciatingly high levels if you've had a previous accident), gasoline costs, emissions testing, license plates, and repairs. Not to mention parking expenses or parking and speeding tickets. Are you certain you want a car?

Jobs

Getting and keeping a job is important for everyone. Having a job increases your self-esteem, gets you up and out every day, lifts your spirits, and best of all, pays the bills. Sometimes young people don't get their dream job right away. CEO of a major company? Broadway musical star? Professional basketball player? However, once you become an adult, almost any job is better than no job at all—Tourette syndrome or no Tourette syndrome. Here are nine tips for that all-important job interview.

- Be on time. In fact, try to arrive a few minutes early. Make a dry run the day before so you won't get lost.

- Dress for success. Don't wear raggedy jeans, a T-shirt, or dirty sneakers to your interview. Males should wear a suit or sport coat and tie. Females should wear a tailored dress or suit.

- Do your homework. A sure way to impress your prospective employer is to know something about the company. If it's a small company, you could drop by and pick up a brochure or other materials from the receptionist. If it's a big firm, you might do the same thing or visit the public library or chamber of commerce, or try the Internet. Don't be afraid to ask intelligent questions about things you have no other way of finding out. Asking a few well-thought-out questions shows interest.

- Role-play your interview. Have a parent or a friend take the part of the interviewer. Practice your answers to the questions you know the interviewer is going to ask. "What skills will you bring to this job?" "What experience have you had in this kind of work?" "What are your strengths?" (Don't brag, but don't be afraid to be positive about accomplishments that show you can contribute something.) "What needs improvement?" (Don't get down on yourself. Refer to these lacks as your "growth areas" and describe how you're working on them.)

➥ Be sure to bring a résumé, unless you've sent it ahead of time. Keep it on the computer and regularly update it.

➥ If possible, schedule the interview during your best time of the day. Some people's tics get worse in the afternoon. Others with sleep problems or medication side effects may feel less clear-headed in the morning.

➥ Be honest. Don't claim to have skills you don't have. If you don't know the answer to a question, it's better to say so; don't try to fake it.

➥ Discuss the job rather than Tourette syndrome. As mentioned earlier, use your own judgment about how much to say. Don't avoid the subject, but don't focus on it either.

➥ Always follow up your interview with a thank-you note.

If you don't get a job you wanted, don't assume it's because of TS. Few people get the first job they apply for. Dust yourself off and go on to the next interview. Don't be afraid to ask why you didn't get the job. The interviewer will no doubt be impressed with your desire to improve your skills.

Take It Slow

Transitions are hard, and some of these challenges may seem overwhelming. Practice now will make life easier later.

Tourette syndrome causes a loss of control in certain areas of life. But there is much of your life that you can control. Try to make choices that will help, not hurt you. The future is yours.

When Someone Close to You Has Tourette Syndrome

If you're a friend or relative of a young person with Tourette syndrome, you've probably already developed your own coping strategies. Compare your ideas with the ideas below.

Stop That!

At times, you may feel like saying to the person with TS, "Why don't you just stop that? It's driving me crazy!" But remember that the person with Tourette syndrome doesn't want to have any part of this condition, didn't bring it on himself or herself, and can't get rid of it. Nothing could have prevented Tourette syndrome, and nothing can cure it. It might get better, or it might get worse. It might go away for a while, but it might come back. Who knows? So there. You're stuck with it and so is he or she, but this person lives with it twenty-four hours a day.

Try these exercises: Blink your eyes seven times while writing a sentence. Smack your lips or clear your throat four times while reading aloud. Keep kicking your leg while you're in a crowded restaurant. Shout out a few bad words in the middle of a piano recital. Experience the crusty stares of those around you. Chances are if you're the sibling or a close friend of a person with Tourette syndrome, you've felt those stares, and you've heard the rude comments. But you don't have to experience those responses regularly. He or she does. If you can feel the frustration of the person with

Tourette syndrome, you will have empathy. Remember that many of the behaviors connected with associated conditions, such as ADHD and OCD, are also out of your friend or family member's control.

Possible Medication Side Effects

Don't forget to consider the possible side effects of medications. Some are known or anticipated, but others may be unpredictable. Be patient and try to help your friend or relative adjust to them.

Ray, age thirteen, had always loved school and had never missed a day. Suddenly, he started feeling sick. When he refused to go to school, his parents wondered if he could be faking. The doctor suggested that Ray cut back on his medication. Although he had to put up with a few more tics, he regained his enthusiasm for school and extracurricular activities.

Fair Treatment for Friends and Relatives

Your friend or relative with TS doesn't want sympathy. He just wants your friendship and understanding—whether or not he says so. He wants you to treat him like you treat everyone else even though he knows he's not quite like everyone else. Cindy, age eighteen, doesn't have TS; she's legally blind. If it's light outside, she can see shapes. She can read with the aid of a magnifying glass. She's fiercely independent. She walks everywhere she can and takes the bus everywhere else. "It drives me crazy," she says, "when someone takes my arm and tries to help me cross the street like I'm some old lady." Cindy doesn't want equal treatment, she just wants fair treatment. She wants to do as much as possible for herself. She wants respect for the unique person she is. That's how most people with Tourette syndrome feel.

Don't Compare

That brings us to another important lesson: Don't compare. Each person in the world is unique. Pardon the cliché, but two people with Tourette syndrome will be as different from each other as night is from day.

Consider the matter of friends. Some young people with Tourette syndrome have many friends; others have only a few. The number of friends people have seems to have little to do with the seriousness of their tic disorders. It's more a matter of personality and self-esteem. Some people are more outgoing than others—tics or no tics. Take Ian, age sixteen, for example. Ian has tics, which he accepts as part of himself. Therefore, everyone else around him accepts them, too.

Mixed Feelings

Joey, age fifteen, says, "My brother Aaron is a pain. He's thirteen, but he acts like he's about five. He has all kinds of weird tics, including these loud noises he makes like a pig snorting. He goes around trying to touch people. I don't like to bring my friends home because he bugs us. My friends understand—they don't want to come over either—so they invite me to their houses. But sometimes I feel sorry for Aaron because he doesn't have that many friends and no one ever invites him over. Then I start to feel guilty because I could just as easily have been the one to get TS."

It's normal to have mixed feelings about your friend or sibling with Tourette syndrome. You're supposed to like her, but sometimes you don't. (She probably doesn't like you all the time either. No one likes anyone all the time.) Sometimes she embarrasses you. Then you feel guilty. Sometimes you wonder if having a sibling with TS is a kind of punishment for you. Your family can't go to movies or restaurants like "normal" families. What are you supposed to do? Hide out in your room? It's not fair!

During the times you're feeling a mixture of anger, shame, sadness, and guilt, talking to someone will help. The talk may be informal—venting to a friend—or formal, such as an appointment or two with a counselor who understands that these feelings are normal. Going to a Tourette syndrome support group with your sibling or friend just once (or more often) might be all you need to put things in perspective.

Another helpful resource, if you can find one in your community, is a Sibshop. The Sibling Support Project, started at Children's Hospital in Seattle, Washington, has spread to other areas of the United States and other countries. Sibshop support groups are for sisters and brothers of young people with all kinds of disabilities. For further information on Sibshops, call (206) 297-6368 or try the Web site at http://www.thearc.org/siblingsupport.

Family Meetings

Try weekly family meetings at a regular time decided on by the family. Make attendance at these meetings mandatory. Some families find that right after dinner on Sundays works best. Get everyone's input regarding time and then stick to it. Let every family member take a turn as leader. Someone else can volunteer to take minutes. Keep the tone upbeat.

> Jack, age fifteen, the person in his family with Tourette syndrome, heard about family meetings from his friend Paul. Jack introduced the idea to his parents and two brothers. They decided to meet as a family every Sunday after church and brunch. Jack offered to act as leader for the first meeting. His mother volunteered as recorder. Jack began the meeting by asking each person to say something nice about every other person in the family. (That was how Paul's family started its meetings.) The group set rules that included (1) careful listening and no interrupting, (2) no criticism of any person, (3) setting an egg timer if anyone went on for more than three minutes, and (4) a request that each person bring one topic to be discussed to each meeting.

Here are some other things to consider for family meetings.

1. Topics might include the following: (a) each person's right to privacy in the family, (b) each child's need to have some of the parents' time, (c) the parents' need to have some time of their own, and (d) responsibility with household chores.

149

2. Some families like to end their meetings by holding hands and saying a prayer or singing a song.

3. Siblings sometimes like to have a "subcommittee" meeting before the regular meeting to make sure they present a united front at the main meeting.

The family meeting can be a good time to emphasize the fact that no one family member is more important than any other member. It can also be a good time for ongoing education about TS, ADHD, OCD, LD, and other associated conditions. Watching a TS video together can open up discussions and questions. Those who understand the reasons behind various behaviors are more likely to be supportive.

One thing everyone needs to know is that the person with Tourette syndrome has a medical condition requiring lots of patience. But your sibling or friend with TS is no more a saint than you are. Sometimes, people with TS use their symptoms in an unhealthy way. Josh used to increase his tics beyond their usual intensity if he wanted to get out of doing something he considered hard or boring. His mom recognized what was going on and refused to give in to him. As he got older, she explained to him her understanding of the dynamics of the situation. Josh saw the proverbial handwriting on the wall. It was all over for his game. Now fifteen, Josh can tell his "manipulation" story to friends and laugh about it.

A result of regular family meetings is increased solidarity. It's too easy to let a stressful condition like Tourette syndrome tear a family apart. But a family that regularly meets, communicates, listens, and does problem solving together is ready for whatever the world throws its way. Sometimes "arrows" from the outside world come from well-meaning people like grandmas and grandpas; aunts, uncles, and cousins; or family friends. These people may propose so-called treatments, such as herbs and vitamins or special diets. They may give unwanted advice and opinions: "Karen, you just need to shape up." "You're letting him get away with murder." "You should take her off sugar." "Why do you have so many problems at your house? I never have any problem with him." They seem to think their ideas are brilliant or a sure cure.

If a person you know has Tourette syndrome, ask him or her what you can do to be helpful. If the person says "nothing," you're off the hook. Just hang in there and enjoy the friendship.

Glossary

AIDS Abbreviation for acquired immunodeficiency syndrome, which may be contracted by sexual intercourse.

amitriptyline The chemical name for Elavil, a tricyclic antidepressant.

antidepressants A group of medications used to treat the "low-down" feelings that keep a person from enjoying life.

attention deficit hyperactivity disorder (ADHD) A condition in which characteristics such as inattention, hyperactivity, and impulsivity are severe enough to interfere with daily living.

auditory processing problem A condition that causes people to have trouble with listening, interpreting, or remembering what they've heard.

behavioral therapy Counseling that focuses on removing self-defeating behaviors.

bipolar disorder A condition in which periods of depression alternate with periods of mania with normal moods in between. Sometimes called manic-depressive disorder.

cannabinoids Chemical compounds that are the active principles of marijuana.

carbamazapine The chemical name for Tegretol, a medication used to treat seizure disorders but also used in the treatment of bipolar disorders.

chronic tic disorder (CTD) A condition involving motor or vocal tics (but not both) lasting longer than one year.

clomipramine The chemical name for Anafranil, a tricyclic antidepressant.

clonidine The chemical name for Catapres, a drug sometimes used to treat Tourette syndrome.

cognitive therapy Counseling that focuses on changing a person's self-defeating thoughts.

compulsions Actions people take in response to irresistible impulses.

convulsive movements Violent, involuntary muscle contractions.

co-occurring condition A disability that exists alongside another condition such as Tourette syndrome. With TS, these conditions may include attention deficit hyperactivity disorder (ADHD), obsessive-compulsive disorder (OCD), learning differences or disabilities (LD), behavioral difficulties, sleep problems, and others. In the medical literature, these are often called comorbid conditions.

coprolalia The involuntary exclamation of inappropriate or obscene words or statements.

copropraxia The involuntary making of obscene gestures; a rare motor tic.

depression A mental condition often treatable with medication and/or psychotherapy. Depression may include deep feelings of sadness, pessimism, poor coping abilities, crying spells, and withdrawal from other people.

desipramine The chemical name for Norpramin, a tricyclic antidepressant.

dietician A professional trained in the management of foods and special diets.

dopamine A neurotransmitter (brain chemical) involved in the transmission of impulses controlling body movements.

DSM-IV The fourth edition of the *Diagnostic and Statistical Manual of Mental Disorders,* published by the American Psychiatric Association and revised periodically.

dyscalculia Difficulty performing mathematical calculations.

dysgraphia A disability that causes difficult-to-read or illegible handwriting.

dyslexia Impairment of the ability to read.

dystonic tic A writhing or twisting body movement; an unusual tic.

echokinesis Involuntary imitation of another person's movement; also called echopraxia.

echolalia Verbal repetition of the last-heard sound; an echoing.

echopraxia Imitation of another person's movement; also called echokinesis.

empathy Deep understanding of another person's feelings.

esophagus The passageway for food between the throat and the stomach.

experiential learning Learning by doing.

family therapy Counseling that focuses on the family as a whole rather than on one individual.

fluoxetine The chemical name for the antidepressant Prozac.

fluvoxamine The chemical name for the antidepressant Luvox.

GED The General Educational Development Test.

genes The chemical building blocks of heredity.

geneticists Scientists who study genes and how they affect heredity.

gesticulations Animated or excited gestures.

grimaces   Tortured or sharp facial expressions indicating feelings such as pain, disgust, or contempt.

guanfacine   The chemical name for Tenex, a medication sometimes used to treat Tourette syndrome and/or tics.

habit-reversal training (HRT)   The learning of a response to counteract a tic.

haloperidol   The chemical name for Haldol, a neuroleptic drug often used to treat Tourette syndrome.

hyperactive   Overly active.

imipramine   The chemical name for Tofranil, a tricyclic antidepressant.

impulsivity   Tendency to act before considering the consequences of one's actions.

inattention   Problems with concentration.

involuntary   Not willed; out of a person's control.

learning difficulties or learning disabilities   A mixed group of conditions that include difficulty in listening, speaking, writing, reading, reasoning, and doing math, probably because of some dysfunction of the central nervous system.

licensed clinical social worker   A person with a master's degree in social work plus extra supervision and training in counseling.

lithium or lithium carbonate   The chemical name for Eskalith, a medication used to treat bipolar disorder.

manic-depressive disorder   See bipolar disorder.

methylphenidate   The chemical name for Ritalin, a stimulant and one of the best-known medications for treating attention deficit hyperactivity disorder.

motor tics   Sudden, purposeless, involuntary movements such as eye blinking.

neuroleptic drugs   Substances that in some people produce a sedating or tranquilizing effect.

neurotransmitters   Body chemicals that carry signals from cell to cell in the brain and between the nerves.

nicotine   A colorless, rapidly acting toxic substance; one of the major contributors to the harmful effects of smoking.

nortriptyline   The chemical name for Pamelor, a tricyclic antidepressant.

obsessions   Recurring thoughts, images, and impulses that a person finds hard to get rid of.

obsessive-compulsive disorder (OCD) A combination of obsessive thoughts and compulsive behaviors that interfere with a person's life.

occupational therapist   An allied health professional who helps people who have limiting conditions cope with daily living activities.

orderly   A hospital attendant who helps transport and care for patients.

palilalia   The repetition of one's own last word; a rare verbal tic.

pancreas   A long, soft gland behind the stomach. The pancreas secretes pancreatic juice and also produces insulin.

paroxetine   The chemical name for the antidepressant Paxil.

PDA   Personal digital assistant.

pediatric neurologist   A doctor who specializes in children's conditions of the nervous system.

pemoline   The chemical name for the stimulant Cylert, a medication used in treating ADHD.

physical therapist   A person licensed in the care and treatment of people with physical limitations and disabilities.

pimozide The chemical name for Orap, a neuroleptic drug used to treat Tourette syndrome.

postural hypotension A feeling of dizziness or light-headedness when standing up.

psychiatrist A medical doctor who specializes in the diagnosis and treatment of emotional disorders.

psychologist A person with specialized training in the testing and counseling of people with mental and emotional disorders.

psychology The science of the mind and its mental processes.

puberty The period of time during which young men and women mature sexually and become capable of having children.

selective serotonin reuptake inhibitors (SSRIs) A group of antidepressants that increase the levels of the neurotransmitter serotonin by preventing its reuptake by the nerve cells.

self-esteem A person's beliefs about his or her worth as a person.

self-talk The things a person says about himself to himself.

sensory tics Feelings that precede tics in some people.

sequencing problems Difficulties in deciding an order in which to do things.

serotonin A neurotransmitter.

sertraline The chemical name for the antidepressant Zoloft.

shadowing Spending a day or more at work with someone who is involved in a career the "shadower" is interested in.

side effects Undesirable reactions to a given medication that may cause so much discomfort that the person stops taking it.

spatial relationship difficulties   Problems with "centering" oneself in space.

stereotypes   Oversimplified and often irrational beliefs.

stigma   A mark of disgrace.

stimulant   Any agent, including medication, that at least temporarily increases activity or alertness.

streptococcus   A type of bacteria or germ.

tai chi   A Chinese martial art and form of meditative exercise with slow, circular, and stretching movements.

tics   Sudden, usually short, involuntary movements (motor tics) or sounds (vocal or verbal tics).

Tourette syndrome   The most serious tic disorder. A neurological condition involving involuntary muscle movement or sounds, lasting more than one year, and causing anguish to the person who has it.

transdermal   A way of delivering medication passing through the skin.

transient   Passing, or lasting only a short time.

transient tic disorder (TTD)   A condition involving single or multiple motor tics lasting less than one year.

tricyclic antidepressant   A group of medications used to treat depression. Tricyclic antidepressants may also decrease symptoms of ADHD.

valproic acid   The chemical name for Depakote, a medication used in the treatment of seizure disorders and also in the treatment of bipolar disorder.

vocal tics   Involuntary sounds, such as throat clearing.

waxing and waning   A coming and going in frequency and severity, which is the usual course of Tourette syndrome.

yoga   A series of postures and breathing exercises designed to achieve control of mind and body.

Where to Go for Help

If you or someone you know has Tourette syndrome with or without co-occurring conditions, you might find the following list helpful. Most of these organizations provide educational materials, and some will refer you to local groups.

Tourette Syndrome

National Institute of Neurological Disorders and Stroke
NIH Neurological Institute
P.O. Box 5801
Bethesda, MD 20824
(800) 352-9424
Web site: http://www.ninds.nih.gov

National Organization for Rare Disorders, Inc. (NORD)
55 Kenosia Avenue
P.O. Box 1968
Danbury, CT 06813-1968
(203) 744-0100
(800) 999-6673 (voice mail only)
e-mail: orphan@rarediseases.org
Web site: http://www.rarediseases.org

Tourette Syndrome Association, Inc. (TSA)
42–40 Bell Boulevard, Suite 205
Bayside, NY 11361-2820
(718) 224-2999
Toll-free help line: (888) 4-TOURET (486-8738)
e-mail: tourette@ix.netcom.com
Web site: http://tsa-usa.org

WE MOVE
Mount Sinai Medical Center
204 West 84th Street
New York, NY 10024
(800) 437-MOV2 (6682)
e-mail: wemove@wemove.org
Web site: http://www.wemove.org

Attention Deficit Disorders

Attention Deficit Disorder Association (ADDA)
1788 Second Street, Suite 200
Highland Park, IL 60035
(847) 432-ADDA (2332)
e-mail: mail@add.org
Web site: http://www.add.org

Attention Deficit Information Network, Inc. (AD-IN)
58 Prince Street
Needham, MA 02494
(781) 455-9895
e-mail: adin@gis.net
Web site: http://www.addinfonetwork.com

Children and Adults with Attention-Deficit Disorders (CHADD)
8181 Professional Place, Suite 201
Landover, MD 20785
(800) 233-4050
e-mail: national@chadd.org
Web site: http://www.chadd.org

Obsessive-Compulsive Disorder

Obsessive-Compulsive Foundation
337 Notch Hill Road
North Branford, CT 06471
(203) 315-2190
e-mail: info@ocfoundation.org
Web site: http://www.ocfoundation.org

Obsessive Compulsive Information Center
Madison Institute of Medicine
7617 Mineral Point Road, Suite 300
Madison, WI 53717
(608) 827-2470
e-mail: mim@miminc.org
Web site: http://www.miminc.org/aboutocic.html

Learning Disabilities

Council for Exceptional Children (CEC)
1110 North Glebe Road, Suite 300
Arlington, VA 22201
(703) 620-3660
(888) CEC-SPED (232-7733)
e-mail: service@cec.sped.org
Web site: http://www.cec.sped.org

The International Dyslexia Association
Chester Building, Suite 382
8600 LaSalle Road
Baltimore, MD 21286-2044
(410) 296-0232
e-mail: info@interdys.org
Web site: http://www.interdys.org

Learning Disabilities Association of America (LDA)
4156 Library Road
Pittsburgh, PA 15234-1349
(412) 341-1515
e-mail: info@ldaamerica.org
Web site: http://www.ldanatl.org

National Center for Learning Disabilities (NCLD)
381 Park Avenue South, Suite 1401
New York, NY 10016
(212) 545-7510
(888) 575-7373
Web site: http://www.ncld.org

Mental Health

American Foundation for Suicide Prevention
120 Wall Street, 22nd Floor
New York, NY 10005
(212) 363-3500
(888) 333-AFSP (2377)
Web site: http://www.afsp.org

Depression and Bipolar Support Alliance
730 North Franklin Street, Suite 501
Chicago, IL 60610-7204
(312) 642-0049
(800) 826-3632
e-mail: arobinson@ndmda.org
Web site: http://www.ndmda.org

Depression and Related Affective Disorders Association
Meyer 3–181
600 North Wolfe Street
Baltimore, MD 21287-7381
(410) 955-4647
e-mail: drada@jhmi.edu
Web site: http://www.drada.org

The Federation of Families for Children's Mental Health
1101 King Street, Suite 420
Alexandria, VA 22314
(703) 684-7710
e-mail: ffcmh@ffcmh.org
Web site: http://www.ffcmh.org

National Alliance for the Mentally Ill (NAMI)
Colonial Place Three
2107 Wilson Boulevard, Suite 300
Arlington, VA 22201
(703) 524-7600
(800) 950-NAMI (6264)
Web site: http://www.nami.org

National Foundation for Depressive Illness,
   Inc. (NAFDI)
P.O. Box 2257
New York, NY 10116
(800) 239-1265
Web site: http://www.depression.org

National Institute of Mental Health
6001 Executive Boulevard, Room 8184, MSC 9663
Bethesda, MD 20892-9663
(301) 443-4513
e-mail: nimhinfo@nih.gov
Web site: http://www.nimh.nih.gov

Yellow Ribbon Suicide Prevention Program
P.O. Box 644
Westminster, CO 80036-0644
(303) 429-3530
e-mail: ask4help@yellowribbon.org
Web site: http://www.yellowribbon.org

General

National Information Center for Children and Youth
   with Disabilities
P.O. Box 1492
Washington, DC 20013
(800) 695-0285
e-mail: nichy@aed.org
Web site: http://www.nichcy.org

National Library Service for the Blind and
    Physically Handicapped
Library of Congress
Washington, DC 20542
(202) 707-5100
(800) 424-8567
Web site: http://www.loc.gov/nls/

Camps

American Camping Association
5000 State Road 67 North
Martinsville, IN 46151-7902
(765) 342-8465
e-mail: sca@acd-camps.org
Web site: http://www.acacamps.org

Or call the Tourette Syndrome Association for names
of camps.

Web Sites

Due to the changing nature of Internet links, the Rosen
Publishing Group, Inc., has developed an online list of
Web sites related to the subject of this book. This site is
updated regularly. Please use this link to access the list:

www.rosenlinks.com/cop/tsotd

For Further Reading

Tourette Syndrome

Brill, Marlene T. *Tourette Syndrome.* Brookfield, CT: Twenty-First Century Books, 2002.

Bruun, Ruth D., and Bertel Bruun. *A Mind of Its Own: Tourette Syndrome: A Story and a Guide.* New York: Oxford University Press, 1994.

Byalick, Marcia. *Quit It.* New York: Delacorte Press, 2002.

Fowler, Rick. *The Unwelcome Companion: An Insider's View of Tourette Syndrome.* Cashiers, NC: Silver Run Publications, 1996.

Handler, Lowell. *Twitch and Shout: A Touretter's Tale.* New York: Dutton, 1998.

Hecht, Daniel. *Skull Session.* New York: Viking, 1998.

Hughes, Susan. *What Makes Ryan Tick? A Family's Triumph Over Tourette Syndrome and Attention Deficit Disorder.* Duarte, CA: Hope Press, 1996.

Kushner, Howard I. *A Cursing Brain? The Histories of Tourette Syndrome.* Cambridge, MA: Harvard University Press, 1999.

Landau, Elaine. *Tourette Syndrome.* New York: Franklin Watts, 1998.

Lethem, Jonathan. *Motherless Brooklyn.* New York: Doubleday, 1999.

Robertson, Mary M., and Simon Baron-Cohen. *Tourette Syndrome: The Facts.* 2nd ed. New York: Oxford University Press, 1998.

Rubio, Gwyn H. *Icy Sparks*. New York: Viking, 1998.

Sacks, Oliver. *An Anthropologist on Mars: Seven Paradoxical Tales*. New York: Alfred A. Knopf, 1995.

Sacks, Oliver. *The Man Who Mistook His Wife for a Hat and Other Clinical Tales*. New York: Summit Books, 1985.

Seligman, Adam W. *Echolalia: An Adult's Story of Tourette Syndrome*. Duarte, CA: Hope Press, 1991.

Shimberg, Elaine F. *Living with Tourette Syndrome*. New York: Simon & Schuster, 1995.

Waltz, Mitzi. *Tourette Syndrome: Finding Answers and Getting Help*. Cambridge, MA: O'Reilly, 2001.

Attention Disorders

Crist, James J. *ADHD—A Teenagers' Guide*. King of Prussia, PA: Center for Applied Psychology, 1996.

Dendy, Chris, and A. Ziegler. *Teenagers with ADD: A Parents' Guide*. Bethesda, MD: Woodbine House, 1995.

Garber, Stephen W. *Beyond Ritalin: Adults with Attention Deficit Disorders, Facts About Medication and Other Strategies for Helping Children, Adolescents, and Adults*. New York: Harper Collins, 1997.

Hallowell, Edward, and John Ratey, M.D. *Driven to Distraction: Recognizing and Coping with Attention Deficit Disorder from Childhood Through Adulthood*. New York: Simon & Schuster, 1995.

Hechtman, Lily, and Gabriella Weiss. *Hyperactive Children Grown Up: ADHD in Children, Adolescents and Adults*. 2nd ed. New York: Guilford Press, 1993.

Kelly, Kate, and Peggy Ramundo. *You Mean I'm Not Lazy, Stupid, or Crazy? A Self-Help Book for Adults with Attention Deficit Disorder.* New York: Fireside Books, 1996.

Martin, Grant. *The Hyperactive Child.* Colorado Springs, CO: Chariot Victor Publishing, 1998.

Morrison, Jaydene. *Coping with ADD/ADHD (Attention Deficit Disorder/Attention Deficit Hyperactivity Disorder).* Rev. ed. New York: The Rosen Publishing Group, 2000.

Nadeau, Kathleen G. *Survival Guide for College Students with ADD or LD.* New York: Magination Press, 1994.

Quinn, Patricia O., M.D., ed. *ADD and the College Student.* New York: Magination Press, 1994.

Quinn, Patricia O., M.D., and Judith M. Stern. *Putting on the Brakes: Young People's Guide to Understanding Attention Deficit Hyperactivity Disorder (ADHD).* New York: Magination Press, 1991.

Obsessive-Compulsive Disorder

Baer, Lee. *Getting Control: Overcoming Your Obsessions and Compulsions.* New York: NAL/Dutton, 1992.

Foa, Edna B., and Reid Wilson. *Stop Obsessing! How to Overcome Your Obsessions and Compulsions.* New York: Bantam Books, 1991.

Gravitz, Herbert L. *Obsessive-Compulsive Disorder: New Help for the Family.* Santa Barbara, CA: Healing Visions Press, 1998.

Griest, John H. *Obsessive-Compulsive Disorder: A Guide.* 6th ed. Madison, WI: Dean Foundation for Health, Research and Education, 1997.

Johnson, Hugh F. *Obsessive-Compulsive Disorder in Children and Adolescents: A Guide.* Rev. ed. Madison, WI: Dean Foundation for Health, Research and Education, 1997.

Penzel, Fred. *Obsessive-Compulsive Disorders: A Complete Guide to Getting Well and Staying Well.* New York: Oxford University Press, 2000.

Rapoport, Judith L., M.D. *The Boy Who Couldn't Stop Washing: The Experience and Treatment of Obsessive-Compulsive Disorder.* New York: E.P. Dutton, 1989.

Spencer, Terry. *Kissing Doorknobs.* New York: Delacorte Press, 1998.

Steketee, Gail, and Kerrin White, M.D. *When Once Is Not Enough: Help for Obsessive-Compulsives.* Oakland, CA: New Harbinger Publications, 1990.

Wilensky, Amy S. *Passing for Normal: A Memoir of Compulsion.* New York: Broadway Books, 1999.

Learning Disabilities

Cummings, Rhoda W. *The School Survival Guide for Kids with LD (Learning Differences): Ways to Make Learning Easier and More Fun.* Minneapolis: Free Spirit Publishing, 1991.

Donnelly, Karen. *Coping with Dyslexia.* New York: The Rosen Publishing Group, 2000.

Fisher, Gary L., and Rhoda Cummings. *Survival Guide for Kids with LD; Learning Differences.* Minneapolis: Free Spirit Publishing, 1990.

Janover, Caroline. *Josh: A Boy with Dyslexia.* Burlington, VT: Waterfront Books, 1998.

Stern, Judith, and Ben-Ami Uzi. *Many Ways to Learn: Young People's Guide to Learning Disabilities.* Washington, DC: American Psychological Association, 1996.

Depression

Bellenir, Karen, ed. *Mental Health Information for Teens: Health Tips about Mental Health and Mental Illness.* Detroit: Omnigraphics, 2001.

Copeland, Mary Ellen, and Stuart Copans, M.D. *The Adolescent Depression Workbook.* Brattleboro, VT: Peach Press, 1998.

Gelman, Amy. *Coping with Depression and Other Mood Disorders.* New York: The Rosen Publishing Group, 2000.

Moe, Barbara. *Coping with Mental Illness.* New York: The Rosen Publishing Group, 2001.

Wesson, Carolyn M. *Teen Troubles: How to Keep Them from Becoming Tragedies.* New York: Walker and Company, 1988.

General

Dornbush, Marilyn P., and Sheryl H. Pruitt. *Teaching the Tiger: A Handbook for Individuals Involved in the Education of Students with Attention Deficit Disorders, Tourette Syndrome or Obsessive-Compulsive Disorders.* Duarte, CA: Hope Press, 1995.

Koplewicz, Harold S., M.D. *It's Nobody's Fault: New Hope for Difficult Children and Their Parents.* New York: Times Books/Random House, 1996.

For Siblings

Klein, Stanley D., and Maxwell J. Schleifer, eds. *It Isn't Fair! Siblings of Children with Disabilities.* Westport, CT: Bergin & Garvey, 1993.

Meyer, Donald J. *Living with a Brother or Sister with Special Needs: A Book for Sibs.* 2nd ed., rev., Seattle: University of Washington Press, 1996.

Meyer, Donald J., ed. *Views from Our Shoes: Growing Up with a Brother or Sister with Special Needs.* Bethesda, MD: Woodbine House, 1997.

College Guides

Kravets, Mary Beth, and Imy F. Wax. *The K and W Guide to Colleges for the Learning Disabled: A Resource Book for Students, Parents, and Professionals.* New York: Random House, 1997.

Mangrum, Charles T., II, and Stephen S. Strichart. *Peterson's Guide to Colleges with Programs for Students with Learning Disabilities or Attention Deficit Disorders.* 5th. ed. Princeton, NJ: Peterson's Guide, 1997.

Videos

After the Diagnosis: The Next Steps. 2001. 35 minutes.

Family Life with Tourette Syndrome . . . Personal Stories: A Six-Part Series. 2001.

I'm a Person Too. 1997. 22 minutes.

Stop It! I Can't. 1997. 13 minutes.

Talking About Tourette Syndrome. 1996. 45 minutes.

Bibliography

American Psychiatric Association. *Diagnostic and Statistical Manual of Mental Disorders.* 4th ed. Washington, DC: American Psychiatric Association, 1994.

Barkley, Russell A. *Attention Deficit Hyperactivity Disorder: A Clinical Workbook.* New York: Guilford Press, 1998.

Berecz, John M. *Understanding Tourette Syndrome, Obsessive Compulsive Disorder, and Related Problems: A Developmental and Catastrophe Theory Perspective.* New York: Springer Publishing Company, 1992.

Bruun, Ruth D., Donald Cohen, and James F. Leckman. *Guide to the Diagnosis and Treatment of Tourette Syndrome.* Bayside, NY: Tourette Syndrome Foundation of Canada, 1998.

Chase, Thomas N., Arnold J. Friedhoff, and Donald J. Cohen, eds. *Tourette Syndrome: Genetics, Neurobiology, and Treatment.* New York: Raven Press, 1992.

Hollander, Eric, et al., eds. *CNS Spectrums: The International Journal of Neuropsychiatric Medicine.* Vol. 4, No. 2, and Vol. 4, No. 3. New York: Medworks Media, 1999.

Hollander, Eric, and Dan J. Stein. *Obsessive-Compulsive Disorders: Diagnosis, Etiology, Treatment.* New York: Dekker, 1997.

King, Robert A., and Lawrence Scahill, eds. *Child and Adolescent Psychiatric Clinics of North America.* Vol. 8, No. 3. Philadelphia: W.B. Saunders Company, 1999.

Kushner, Howard I. *A Cursing Brain? The Histories of Tourette Syndrome.* Cambridge, MA: Harvard University Press, 1999.

Leckman, James F., and Donald Cohen. *Tics, Obsessions, Compulsions: Developmental Psychopatholgy and Clinical Care.* New York: John Wiley & Sons, 1999.

Martin, Andres, and Lawrence Scahill, eds. *Child and Adolescent Psychiatric Clinics of North America.* Vol. 9, No. 1. Philadelphia: W.B. Saunders Company, 1999.

Robertson, Mary M., and Simon Baron-Cohen. *Tourette Syndrome: The Facts.* 2nd ed. New York: Oxford University Press, 1998.

Index

About the Author

Barbara Moe, R.N., M.S.N., M.S.W., is a nurse, a social worker, and a writer with an interest in helping young people conquer life challenges. She is the author of several other books published by the Rosen Publishing Group, including *Coping with Eating Disorders, Coping as a Survivor of a Violent Crime, Coping with PMS, Coping with Bias Incidents, Coping with Mental Illness*, and *Coping with Rejection*.

Acknowledgments

I appreciate the help of Paul Moe, M.D.; Dani Arck, J.D.; Cathy LeGrand, M.L.S.; The Children's Hospital of Denver Library; The Denver Library; the Tourette Syndrome Association, Inc.; and the Rocky Mountain Region Tourette Syndrome Association, Inc. A special thanks to all of those who shared their stories.

Layout: Tom Forget; **Editor:** Mark Beyer